Cambridge Elements

Elements in Indigenous Environmental Research
Series Editors
Dina Gilio-Whitaker
California State University San Marcos
Clint R. Carroll
University of Colorado Boulder
Joy Porter
University of Birmingham

Associate Editor
Matthias Wong
National University of Singapore

"ALASKA" IS NOT A BLANK SPACE

Unsettling Aldo Leopold's Odyssey

Julianne Warren
Independent Scholar

Shaftesbury Road, Cambridge CB2 8EA, United Kingdom

One Liberty Plaza, 20th Floor, New York, NY 10006, USA

477 Williamstown Road, Port Melbourne, VIC 3207, Australia

314–321, 3rd Floor, Plot 3, Splendor Forum, Jasola District Centre, New Delhi – 110025, India

103 Penang Road, #05–06/07, Visioncrest Commercial, Singapore 238467

Cambridge University Press is part of Cambridge University Press & Assessment, a department of the University of Cambridge.

We share the University's mission to contribute to society through the pursuit of education, learning and research at the highest international levels of excellence.

www.cambridge.org
Information on this title: www.cambridge.org/9781009476034

DOI: 10.1017/9781009384728

© Julianne Warren 2025

This publication is in copyright. Subject to statutory exception and to the provisions of relevant collective licensing agreements, no reproduction of any part may take place without the written permission of Cambridge University Press & Assessment.

When citing this work, please include a reference to the DOI 10.1017/9781009384728

First published 2025

A catalogue record for this publication is available from the British Library

ISBN 978-1-009-47603-4 Hardback
ISBN 978-1-009-38475-9 Paperback
ISSN 2755-0826 (online)
ISSN 2755-0818 (print)

Cambridge University Press & Assessment has no responsibility for the persistence or accuracy of URLs for external or third-party internet websites referred to in this publication and does not guarantee that any content on such websites is, or will remain, accurate or appropriate.

For EU product safety concerns, contact us at Calle de José Abascal, 56, 1°, 28003 Madrid, Spain, or email eugpsr@cambridge.org.

"Alaska" Is Not a Blank Space

Unsettling Aldo Leopold's Odyssey

Elements in Indigenous Environmental Research

DOI: 10.1017/9781009384728
First published online: August 2025

Julianne Warren
Independent Scholar
Author for correspondence: Julianne Warren, coyotetrail.net@pm.me

Abstract: This Element supports Gwich'in, Iñupiat, and all Alaska Natives' collective continuance and reparative justice from the perspective of a settler in the traditional territories of lower Tanana Dene Peoples. It stands with Alaska Natives' recovering and safe-keeping: kinships obstructed by settler-colonialism; ontologies and languages inseparable from land-relations and incommensurable with English-language perspectives; and epistemologies not beholden to any colonialist standard. These rights and responsibilities clash with Leopoldian conservation narratives still shaping mind-sets and institutions that eliminate Indigenous Peoples by telling bad history and by presuming entitlements to lands and norm-making authority. It models an interlocking method and methodology – surfacing white supremacist settler-colonialist assumptions and structures of Leopoldian conservation narratives – that may be adapted to critique other problematic legacies. It offers a praxis of anti-colonialist, anti-racist, liberatory environmental-narrative critical-assessment centering Indigenous experts and values, including consent, diplomacy, and intergenerational respect needed for stable coalitions-making for climate and socio-environmental justice.

Keywords: decolonization, Alaska Native sovereignty, Aldo Leopold, environmental justice, land ethics

© Julianne Warren 2025

ISBNs: 9781009476034 (HB), 9781009384759 (PB), 9781009384728 (OC)
ISSNs: 2755-0826 (online), 2755-0818 (print)

Contents

1 Introduction: Facing Decolonization   1

2 Matrix of Methodology and Method   27

3 Refusing Leopoldian Settler-Colonial Proposals   39

4 Self-Critiquing Rote Repetition (A Redux)   85

5 Settler Listening as Rejoinder: Alaska Native Storytelling   88

6 Conclusion: Toward Kinship   105

References   109

1 Introduction: Facing Decolonization

When I moved from Lenapehoking New York City to Lower Tanana Dene Lands Fairbanks, Alaska, I moved from one educational-activist community into another. Initially, Fairbanks Climate Action Coalition meetings felt familiar compared with those of NYU Divest!, part of a growing Fossil Fuel Divestment Movement.[1] In both places there were many young people studying and co-creating theories of change, leading trainings in non-violent protest, and trying to make spaces safe for those on the frontlines of land protection and environmental justice. There were plenty of strategic planning sessions with white boards and markers and flow-charts, and plenty of story-sharing. In Fairbanks, however, I participated in my first decolonization and Indigenous advocacy workshops. These were offered by the Native-led organizations Native Movement and the Gwich'in Steering Committee, encouraging more stable alliances with non-Native groups.[2]

The Gwich'in Steering Committee was established in 1988 after Gwich'in elders convened a gathering during which the Nation resolved to speak as one voice against oil and gas drilling in Iizhik Gwats'an Gwandaii Goodlit The Sacred Place Where Life Begins. This is the birthing ground of the Porcupine Caribou Herd, inseparable from the Gwich'in. The Committee also would educate non-Gwich'in people on reasons to protect this Land tied with Gwich'in life because, as Neets'aii Gwich'in spokesperson Sarah James says, "oil is huge" and "we can't do it by ourself" (BLM, 2019a :8). The coastal plain (and beyond) is land never ceded by Gwich'in or Iñupiat to Russia or to the United States. Since 1960, the U.S. has claimed this geography as the 1002 area, taking its one and a half million acres as part of the Arctic National Wildlife Refuge. While 8 million acres of the 19.6 million acre Refuge were designated "wilderness," the coastal plain, in 1980, was excluded from this stronger protection as a political concession to the petroleum industry. This set up the ongoing fight over the plain's future. The history of Arctic Refuge advocacy and non-Natives' need for Gwich'in-led education are entangled with well-meaning settler-colonialist notions and on-the-ground expressions of wilderness as well as industry (Dunaway, 2021; Warren, 2024).[3]

Aldo Leopold (1887–1948) was a co-founder of The Wilderness Society in 1935. He had already published several writings developing the idea and values of wilderness and rationales for bounding areas protected from "the hammer of

---

[1] www.sunrisenyu.org/divest.
[2] https://ourarcticrefuge.org; www.nativemovement.org; https://fairbanksclimateaction.org.
[3] For a timeline see Dunaway, F. (2023). *Defending the Arctic Refuge: A Book and Public History Site*, https://defendingthearcticrefuge.com/timeline/.

development" (1935: 6) with influence still echoing in the 1964 U.S. Wilderness Act. Leopold was credited by the Society's first president, National Parks Association founder Robert Sterling Yard (1861–1945), as responsible for "starting the idea and title of the wilderness area."[4] Leopold had "first spread it broadcast," beginning with establishing the first wilderness area in the U.S. Forest Service (Flader 1991, 1994; Warren, 2008: 101). National Park Service Planner George Collins, one of the key strategists envisioning what would become the Arctic Refuge, in 1999, also credited Leopold's influence. "It was [Leopold's] ideas we brought to Alaska," he said. "If he hadn't lived I don't think the Arctic Refuge would be what it is today" (Kaye, 2006: 30).

Leopold had begun his career in the USFS in 1909 and otherwise influenced its scientific land-management policies from its earliest days.[5] He also authored *Game Management* (1933), the first major textbook developing this field. In 1947, Leopold served as president of the Ecological Society of America, who particularly wished him to help harmonize concerns shared with wilderness lovers. Leopold's ideas are at the foundation of the U.S. scientific conservation legacy. They also have influenced the contemporary environmental movement and agrarianism in the U.S. Leopold's most well-known work is his posthumously published *A Sand County Almanac* (1949), featuring his "land ethic" pointing to his ecologically informed vision of "land health." The *Almanac* became, in Wallace Stegner's words, "a famous, almost holy book in conservation circles" (Savoy, 2016: 32), gaining popularity around the first "Earth Day" in 1970. About the same time, prominent contemporary agrarians were rooting in Leopoldian ideas and grand narratives, including Wes Jackson, founder of The Land Institute. Leopold, says Jackson, "recognized the *problem of agriculture*," which his Institute is intent upon solving (Jackson, 2011: 30; see also Hausdoerffer, et al., 2021: 145–153). In 2020, in celebration of the fiftieth anniversary of Earth Day, Oxford University Press issued a new edition of Leopold's *Almanac* with an introduction by acclaimed author and conservationist Barbara Kingsolver. Within a year, tens of thousands of readers purchased the volume. Translated from English into fourteen other languages, Leopold's *A Sand County Almanac* had already sold millions of copies worldwide.

In mostly academic circles, I had felt defensive of Leopold. As I continued learning from Alaska Native colleagues, standing with them in defense of their lands and justice, however, I became increasingly uncomfortable about my authorship of a book developing and disseminating Leopold's ecological-ethical ideas of proper human relationships within land communities. Not

---

[4] For more on the National Parks construction of uninhabited, virgin wilderness for Indigenous dispossession see Gilio-Whitaker, 2019: 92–94, Spence, 1999.
[5] For biographies see Flader, 1994, Meine, 2010, Lorbiecki, 2016, Warren, 2016.

only could I *not* imagine my Fairbanks colleagues reading it, I cringed at the thought. At first I had wanted to hide, and certainly no longer to defend my past work. Thanks to the educational labor of my Indigenous colleagues, I was beginning to understand how not only offensive but dangerous conservation, including Leopoldian conservation, was, and is. So, too, then, were my own writings, focused on "land health." These had not pointed out that Leopoldian narratives – while critiquing the dominating U.S. culture of bad land-use, including forms of conservation that would be "too little too late" (Flader and Callicott, 1991: 295) – nonetheless did not break from the power structures of the society expressing it. And "the thread from which the American social fabric is woven," says Colville Confederated Tribes citizen and scholar Dina Gilio-Whitaker, is "white supremacy" (2019: 99).

By "white supremacy" Gilio-Whitaker does not mean an ideology restricted to "rogue alt-right neo-Nazis or white nationalist fringe groups." Nor does she use the term to describe only "hostile behavior from which individuals can excuse themselves" because they are friendly to or even live with a person of color. As Gilio-Whitaker says, "white supremacy" is "a foundational worldview constructed by centuries of white European settlement of the United States" (99). This worldview structures privileges for Europeans self-racialized as white – and, "beyond phenotype," to those legitimated by this legacy of power (Tuck and Yang, 2012: 5; Tallbear, 2013: 136–141) – while it dehumanizes, oppresses, and eliminates people racialized and looked down on as not-white, including "American Indians, African Americans, and ethnic minority 'others'" (Gilio-Whitaker, 2019: 99). Racialized oppressions intersect with related versions of authority and control, such as heteropatriarchy and ableism. In this sense, writing as a structurally privileged member of a white supremacist Nation reinforcing and not undermining systemic injustices to Indigenous, Black and Brown people/s, as well as in exhibiting "hostile behavior" or overt racism in some instances, Aldo Leopold's narratives are white supremacist. As a woman, I am personally beset by patriarchy. At the same time, I, too, continually perpetuate white supremacy in terms of built-in privileges and still unlearned oppressive assumptions, while more recently struggling to be part of undermining it and supporting environmental, which is also social, justice with entwined liberation called for in the short and long terms (Memmi, 1965).[6]

The legacy of white supremacy is enmeshed with that of U.S. settler-colonialism. This is the context of Leopold's conservation narratives and

---

[6] Thanks to Kyle Whyte for introducing me to Memmi's work. Memmi discusses how "In the eyes of the colonized, all Europeans in the colonies are *de facto* colonizers, and whether they want to be or not, they are colonizers in some ways" (1965: 130).

thus of this Element, although others might be able to elaborate and connect the praxis encouraged here to assessments beyond this American location. "White" Euro-Americans' imperial legacy is one of self-righteous theft of non-European lands via a doctrine of Christian discovery. Christian discovery was first sanctioned by fifteenth-century Papal Bulls and, as recently as March 2023, was repudiated by the Vatican. This policy meant that European explorers of often vying Empires – including the French, British and Spanish – who landed in geographies inhabited by non-Christians – including many Indigenous Nations – could claim these lands in the name of their sovereigns by presumed right of divinely sanctioned superiority (Gilio-Whitaker, 2019: 25, 55–56; also Dunbar-Ortiz, 2014; Estes, 2019; Hernandez, 2022). In 1823, the U.S. Supreme Court, via the *Johnson v M'Intosh* decision, first wove the discovery doctrine into property law giving the U.S. superior right of land title. This became part of a series of other federal decisions to justify, within its new and growing empire, ongoing violence and land theft from culturally and politically self-determining Indigenous Peoples. Many Indigenous Peoples long pre-existed U.S. occupation and had track records of innovative technologies and re/generational land relations (Kimmerer, 2013; Whyte, 2015, 2024; Kolopenuk, 2020).[7] As Europeans usurped North American lands, they not only colonized but also settled them, building infrastructure, spreading westward under manifest destiny.

That is, "settler colonialism," as defined by scholars Eve Tuck (Unangax̂) and K. Wayne Yang (U.S.), is when "settlers come with the intention of making a new home on the land, a homemaking that insists on settler sovereignty over all things in their new domain" (2012: 5). And, as these authors underscore, citing Australian scholar Patrick Wolfe (1999), "settler colonialism is a structure and not an event." Incorporated into this structure is the labor stolen from chattel slaves required for successful European dominion over stolen geographies and extraction of economic "resources" from them. White settler-colonialism (1) relegates Indigenous Peoples and others racialized as non-white from customary geographies, disrupting their co-constituted relationships, including by killing; (2) appropriates lands and labor from their people; and (3) assimilates everyone into empire's all-inclusive appetites. As a structure of relationships, functioning as a system expressing a normative worldview, the genocidal violence of settler-colonialism is not merely located in the past; it is very much still present, visible in the consequences of intensifying climate warming. To date, as U.S.-based scholar Farhana Sultana says,

---

[7] Gilio-Whitaker, D. (2022). "Environmental Justice Is Only the Beginning," www.hcn.org/issues/54.7/indigenous-affairs-perspective-environmental-justice-is-only-the-beginning.

"common climate narratives are often about white futures that 'de-future' racialized Others which reinforces white supremacy" (2022: 8).[8]

Sultana's observation applies to common, contemporary Leopoldian conservation narratives. With few exceptions (e.g., Cryer, 2015; Powell 2015, 2016; Cook and Sheehey, 2020) white settler philosophers, scientists, and Leopold scholars, including myself, have "revisited" Leopold's work in order to defend, uplift, expand, reinterpret, and/or lightly critique it and/or others' interpretations of it (Millstein, 2015; Rolston, 2015; Meine, 2022).[9] For instance, in a 2011 U.S. National Endowment for the Humanities Summer Institute titled, "Rethinking the Land Ethic: The Humanities and Sustainability," my own lecture series looked "through the lens" of Leopold's land health concept to explore a Western legacy of utopias and consider what were desired and possible futures. In the process, I critiqued my own heritage of ideas, including some of Leopold's earlier ones, yet without ever questioning the structures of power within nor the ongoing authority of either. So far, questioning by Euro-settler scholars of racism and colonialism in Leopoldian narratives and of his canonical importance to any desired future has been limited.

This trend has been changing. Recently, in one of the few exceptions, philosophers Anna Cook (second generation Canadian) and Bonnie Sheehey (U.S.-based) have critiqued Leopold's historical-evolutionary narrative of ethical extension from humans to land. Although Leopold's narrative focuses on human-land interdependencies, they note, ironically, it "laminates" delocalized Greco-European perspectives over localized Indigenous relationships, thus projecting a "normativity" that is "groundless," assimilative, eliminatory, expansionary, and harmful (Coulthard & Simpson, 2016; Cook & Sheehey, 2020). These authors also reflect on the observation of Citizen Potawatomi philosopher Kyle Powys Whyte that Leopold's historical-ethical narrative of progress "unfolds in the opposite direction" of the narratives many Indigenous

---

[8] For a brief discussion, see Trahant, M. (2019). "How Colonization of the Americas Killed 90 Percent of Their Indigenous People – And Changed the Climate, www.yesmagazine.org/opinion/2019/02/13/how-colonization-of-the-americas-killed-90-percent-of-their-indigenous-people-and-changed-the-climate. There is a vast literature/s by Indigenous and other frontlines authors related to un/desired futures (including the already present one/s) e.g., Whyte, 2017 a and b, 2018b; Davis and Todd, 2017; Ybarra, 2022. Also Espelie, E., et al. (2020–21). *Deep Horizons: Making Visible an Unseen Spectrum of Ecological Casualties and Prospects*, www.colorado.edu/project/environmental-futures/. And, in my community, Alaska Just Transition, *Remembering Forward: Just Transition*, www.justtransitionak.org.

[9] Also Forbes, W. (2017). "Revisiting the 'River of the Mother of God,'" https://humansandnature.org/revisiting-the-river-of-the-mother-of-god/; Colwell, et al. (2014). "Revisiting Leopold: Resource Stewardship in the National Parks," http://parksjournal.com/wp-content/uploads/2014/10/PARKS-20.2-Colwell-et-al-10.2305IUCN.CH_.2014.PARKS-20-2.DRC_.en_.pdf, (Revisits the 1963 *Leopold Report*, chaired by Aldo's son Starker).

people would provide (Whyte, 2015: 2, 2024).[10] They expound on how this narrative "does not account for the role of power in conditioning settler history and ethical relations (348–349)." The quotation of Whyte's is from his paper "How Similar Are Indigenous and North American Environmental Ethics," which he wrote subsequent to the NEH Summer Institute, where we first met. Whyte's original essay was supposed to appear in a collection that was never published. On SSRN, it has been downloaded over 1500 times, in any case. A somewhat revised version (in 2024) is now slated for another volume.

Whyte's piece was prompted by the sometimes agitated, defensive, or even hostile insistence, "in academic or in conservation and climate action circles," of the necessity to compare Indigenous and Leopoldian ethics. Some non-Indigenous colleagues even have asked Whyte to line up his own ethical work with others' interpretations of Leopold's (2024). Meanwhile, as Leopold scholars were "fussing over Leopold's reputation," Whyte writes, "massive environmental injustices against Indigenous peoples were occurring" (2024). Moreover, Leopold's writings do not speak to matters important to many Indigenous people or to the roles of their own ethics, Whyte explains (2015, 2024). Meaning to engage with those at least trying to listen, Whyte looked in the literature for serious attempts to compare North American Indigenous and Leopoldian ethics. From that study, he proposed three crucial issues that – left unaddressed in any further comparisons – would overlook crucial differences and perpetuate coalition-destabilizing Indigenous suppression in (1) history-telling, (2) consequential ethical abstractions, and (3) assumed epistemologies (2015, 2024). As a Leopold scholar, in this Element my method is to more comprehensively interpret Leopoldian texts and to organize a rejoinder, which is listening to understand particular Alaska Native perspectives, according to all three of Whyte's crucial issues. This Element, in Cook and Sheehey's terms, "accounts for the role of power" harmfully normalized throughout Leopoldian narratives (2020: 336). My desire is to support development of a praxis of "deep narrative and ontological revision" of a settler worldview, in the words of the Sisseton-Wahpeton Oyate scholar Kim Tallbear, by my re-delving into Leopold's influential thinking and story-telling (2019: 36).

---

[10] Whyte's essay "How Similar Are Indigenous North American and Leopoldian and Environmental Ethics" was first drafted as an invited essay for an edited volume. This was subsequent to a Leopold-focused event in which Whyte had participated. Whyte posted his draft, in 2012, on the SSRN platform followed by a 2015 revision (https://papers.ssrn.com/sol3/papers.cfm?abstract_id=2022038). Publication of the original edited volume was then delayed until 2017, and then never happened. Understanding it to be forthcoming in 2017, however, Whyte also posted the paper on ResearchGate. Altogether, it has had thousands of reads. More recently, Whyte's essay was invited into another edited volume, which, to date, is in progress. Whyte has a 2024 revised version (unpaginated) prepared for this new volume. As called for, I will cite either or both the 2015 and 2024 versions. (with his consent; thank you, again, Kyle).

The most prominent of settler scholars revisiting Leopoldian narratives is historian and Leopold biographer Curt Meine. Meine has continued lightly critiquing, defending, and keeping Leopold centered, most recently in his comprehensive 2022 article "Land, ethics, justice, and Aldo Leopold." As a long-term Aldo Leopold Foundation Senior Fellow, Meine's writing also has developed alongside the work of the Aldo Leopold Foundation, intending to "foster a land ethic through the legacy of Aldo Leopold" (https://www.aldoleopold.org/about/mission-and-vision). The Foundation's 2021 online speaker series "Land Ethics and Social Justice: Building an Ethic of Care," to which Meine contributed, for instance, featured white and non-white participants with a platform wide-reaching enough to have drawn 3,387 registered participants, representing every U.S. state and over 11 countries.[11] This juxtaposition, of keeping Leopold centered while talking about racial inclusion, diversity, engagement, and/or justice, sheds light on how these things are not necessarily the same as deep ontological and narrative revisioning. At the same time, it bears hope that any unearthed contradictions may lead to increasingly strategic, supportive direct action for environmental justice and caring. This juxtaposition also sheds light on the often complex and of course non-homogeneous positionalities of non-white thinkers, including some with engagements with Leopold's legacy that are positive, or potentially so.

One speaker in the 2021 event was the Black American ornithologist J. Drew Lanham. He is author of *The Home Place: Memoirs of a Colored Man's Love Affair with Nature* and many other writings, including an essay for *Audubon Magazine* grappling with the racist legacy of John James Audubon (2021).[12] In the form of a letter "to my dear Estella, Jr. [Leopold's youngest daughter]," Lanham raises many questions. His is a poetic reckoning with his childhood adoption of "your dad, Aldo, as my own" – as Leopold was "one who cannot live without wild things words . . . stuck like cockleburs" (2021: 13:00) – in the "raw" aftermath of Lanham's own father's death. Lanham acknowledges that connecting with a dead, white privileged author "is a risky business" (13:00). He wonders how "Aldo would have felt about me [a Black man], about . . . the societal sins of racism and bigotry and all the other biases." "Does his kindness to and through you," Estella, he asks, does kindness from throughout Leopold family who are warmly hosting him, "is all of that a good enough predictor of a rising tide of ideas that weren't of his time but in actuality beyond it? Can we

---

[11] "Why Words from the Land Matter," Last accessed, 2023–4, www.aldoleopold.org/about/land-ethics-and-social-justice/. Please contact The Aldo Leopold Foundation for information on the apparently since archived video.

[12] Lanham, J.D. (2021). "What Do We Do About John James Audubon?" www.audubon.org/magazine/spring-2021/what-do-we-do-about-john-james-audubon.

take the words we know now as uninformed or biased, he made in his imperfections, in context of his greater human whole?" In response, Lanham hears Estella arguing "for inclusion at every level of this [conservation] work, [echoing from her father's advice], 'just do the right thing'" (31:00). And Lanham hears Estella affirming that her "dad was who I had believed him to be, a kind patient man, a lover of his family and the land," imperfect, yes, "but with a vision that broadened out in this wide, rich fan of thinking" (15:00). Leopold, he continues, also had a mind "led by a heart that seemed to be bigger than those of his compatriots" (27:00). Lanham asks, "what's the legacy left behind?" (26:00). He finds in Leopold's daughter Estella "a bright light and enduring legacy that allows me to see the evolution of care in the flesh of someone I never knew" (34:00). At the same time, Lanham acknowledges that many questions arose, for him, that "go unresolved." And, too, he says, there is "ultimately the reckoning that each of us must have with our heroes and with history" (45:00). It is my own earnest reckoning, as a white settler and Leopold scholar, that I respectfully offer in this Element.

Lauret Savoy, geologist and woman of African-, Euro-, and Native American heritage, has been another guest of the Aldo Leopold Foundation. Savoy is author of *Trace: Memory, History, Race, and the American Landscape* (2015) and many other path-making writings, including a 2023 essay for *Emergence Magazine* exposing the construction of race in America. In *Trace*, Savoy's perspective on Leopold also involves the warmth of relations within the present-day Leopold community and an adult reckoning. She looks back on her fourteen-year-old self first reading *A Sand County Almanac*. She had been attracted by Leopold's "intimate images of land" and "the seeming openness of this man's struggle to frame personal truth" (33). At the same time, Savoy "so feared" that Leopold's albeit expansive "we" did not include her and others "with ancestral roots in Africa, Asia, or Native America" (33–34). Years later, gifted by the Foundation with time by the Wisconsin River, Savoy finds herself standing on "worn-out" farmland that Leopold and his family had begun restoring. She imagines the possibility not only of the "capacity for self-renewal" that is the "health of the land" but also, correspondingly, "the health of the human family" with an "intergenerational capacity for locating ourselves within many inheritances" (2015: 47). Along this path, she also wants *A Sand County Almanac* to meet a novel published the same year – *Alien Land*, which was written by her father Willard Savoy. She wants these two narratives which have yet "to meet and answer to each other" to do so in our lifetimes (47). *Alien Land* powerfully conveys fear, grief, and anger from singular and systemic, racialized violence against African Americans also loss of personal dignity – also deeply rooted in losses of land relationships. Her father's book portrays a struggle, across a lifetime, to regain dignity in an unjustly divided world (Savoy, 1949; Savoy 2015: 48). "Yet who else," Savoy writes in *Trace*, "then or now, would put these books on the same shelf?" (39). Without this meeting of narratives, without hearing their clashes reverberate as well as resonances, to my understanding, will, paradoxically, risk capture in the "separate trap," in Savoy's words. It will risk repeating "inculcated divisions" of skin types and of human beings and land relations. Without recognizing "who and what *we* are," there is danger of sticking ineffectually between theory and practice and of losing responsibility and respect to disingenuous and even well-meaning gestures (43–44).

There is also the danger, when theory and practice do not keep up with one another, of even well-meaning demanding actions not accomplishing their intention, reinscribing harms. Consider the "we" who "identify as non-Indigenous, white, and privileged," in Whyte's words, having gained by historic and ongoing oppressions of the Indigenous and/or Black and/or more groups with whom we wish to ally.[13] Our ideas have brought us to the desire to enact justice and care. Our acts may include community seed collection gatherings to restore prairies; support for distribution of money from multi-million-dollar conservation organizations to sovereign Tribes and Black land projects and defunding police; and participating in decolonial (Land Back) campaigns against the fossil fuel industry.[14] Caring acts and the relationships built, in turn, might be goods in themselves and also challenge we settler participants' fantastical, ancestral assumptions and institutions of privilege, which, when threatened, might trigger our retreat or move us forward. Challenges to our privilege would need to include, I think, questioning Leopold's suggestion, which Savoy mentions with generosity (44), that "to strive" is "the important thing" because ideals like "justice or liberty for people" are assumed to be as unattainable as expectations of "harmony with land." Not merely striving but achieving, however, appear critical in view of Indigenous and Black peoples' experiences on the front lines of land dispossession, including by conservation interests, and on the front lines of colonialist-imposed mining and polluted waters.

Deepening settler-ontological change needed for increasingly stable coalitions will require more than what is merely imaginable to our settler selves

---

[13] Whyte, K. (2018). "White Allies, Let's Be Honest About Decolonization," www.yesmagazine.org/issue/decolonize/2018/04/03/white-allies-lets-be-honest-about-decolonization.

[14] Respectively, Meine, C. (2020). "Healing Sacred Earth," https://humansandnature.org/healing-sacred-earth/; Hausdoerffer, J. (2020). "What Does an Anti-Racist Wilderness Look Like," https://wilderness-society.org/what-does-an-anti-racist-wilderness-look-like/; Warren, personal experience.

(Tallbear, 2019). It will require a particularly self-aware, non-defensive openness to what we have been suppressing and whom we oppress – and to *not* knowing (Robinson, 2020: 64) – to shift baselines and power relations. It will take a willingness to let go of what are only seeming likenesses between "ethical" conservation (and other settler movements), including Leopoldian narratives, and Indigenous (and other suppressed) ones (Whyte, 2015, 2024). The possibility of stable coalitions of colonizers and colonized intending to overturn that dichotomy will require dispensing with comforting notions of common histories and experiences – a willingness not only to remake but to jettison cherished ideals like wilderness, philanthropy, and our own trustworthiness – and banishing a dream that "we" can get back to our "normal" lives after (or even before) the end of a project or fight. Stabilizing Indigenous-settler alliances-in-action calls for attuning our settler abstractions not only to commonality but to differences that make a difference.

In "Land, Ethics, Justice, and Aldo Leopold" (2022), Meine, undoubtedly well-meaning in his awareness of the urgency of reckoning with injustice in "conservation and the environmental movement" (168), yet maintains, a Leopold-defensive penchant for commonality without also attending to differences required to advance deep, structural revisioning of settler-colonial theory and practices. A "land ethic," Meine writes, "(however labeled)," for Leopold, "was not static and *could not be* exclusionary" (2022: 167, 179). He stresses Leopold's ethic's "core tenets of ecological interdependency," which "explicitly embraced people" with "no conditions" into land community membership. Meine thus takes Leopold's expansionary ethic to "inherently subvert racist, classist, sexist, and white supremacist attitudes" (2022: 167, 179). Such an ethic, Meine claims, "may now contribute to further progress in realizing an ethic of care" (179). "In the broad arc of Western conservation history," Meine says, "the land ethic represented a move away from a colonial and anthropocentric view ... toward something more aligned with Indigenous views" (179). Assuming Leopold as an "essential transitional figure"[15] – even as "within a still broader, ongoing movement, informed by an ever-evolving ethic of care" (167, 180) – with a Leopoldian ethic as an unfolding, bridging, inclusive call for participation (169, 176) veers dangerously close to Whyte's "translational view," which would continue privileging Leopoldian ideas as the basis of

---

[15] With regard to Leopold as "an essential transitional figure," (Meine, 2022: 167, 180) other questions worth raising include: If so, for whom? The assumption that "mainstream American society" would be worse off without Leopold's "new foundations for the expansion of environmental awareness" (Meine 2022: 167) neglects, side by side, to wonder who is worse off because of it? And it neglects to question whether or how, as Leopold wrote, competition between Indigenous, e.g., Puebloan and Euro-American settler cultures for land "was inevitable?" (Flader and Callicott, 1991: 102).

a potential unity of different ethics. Claiming Leopoldian ethics to be moving toward Indigenous views, at the same time, veers dangerously close to Whyte's "convergence view," which would assume similarities of thought among them without warranted skepticism. Holding either view would paper over crucial differences between Leopoldian and many Indigenous perspectives, continuing to suppress the latter and, again, to destabilize environmental justice coalition-making (Whyte, 2015: 3, 2024). Ironically, a Leopoldian narrative of inclusion and alignment could counter shared interest in the habitable Earth everyone does need in common.

At the same time, Meine does acknowledge some of Whyte's cautions against granting unwarranted parallels and privileges to Leopoldian narratives. He supports Whyte's call to "'push beyond linking abstract ideas' and focus on 'bringing together ... people who subscribe to ... different ethics [for] more careful consideration of potential differences'" (Meine, 2022: 175; see Whyte, 2015: 15, 7; 2024). "The moment is ripe for such consideration of contrasting ethical foundations, frameworks, aims, trajectories, and implications for environmental stewardship," Meine says (175). Meine also acknowledges that "the scrutiny being given to Leopold," and historic others, "will, and must, continue" (180). And while Meine allows for Leopold's "ethical blind spots" pertaining to "race and social justice" (169), it appears that, having "evolved across his lifetime" in expansionary ways and in pointing the way there in advancing an "ethic of care," he is not held much responsible (169, 173). More crucially, I do not find deep critique of Leopold's legacy of work that carries forward proposals from his coming of "age in a time, and within a dominant culture," in Meine's words, "marked by systemic racism, classism, and sexism" (169). Yet this dominant culture is, in fact, defined by these marks, to date. That Leopold critiqued his culture's consumer-capitalist greed, for instance, without threatening its white supremacist, colonialist status quo raises questions important for those wishing to do so. "The work of self-scrutiny applies to the present as well," Meine continues, including "in our own lives." Yet, if any of us are to counter, as Meine puts it, the "same elements of racism and injustice" (180) from the past in ourselves – within the still-dominating system – we must surface and face, in order to sort out and refuse, if not the Euro-American settler ancestors per se, the troubling inheritances they've bequeathed.

To go beyond inclusivity, beyond bringing diverse people together, which might create spaces for scrutiny yet not necessarily facilitate it, in this Element – as a settler, as a life-long ecological thinker, writer, activist, and Leopold scholar – I attend to surfacing and unraveling threads of white supremacy in Leopoldian narratives in ways that I also have left undone. In addition, I amplify localized ethical perspectives of Alaska Native persons for "more careful consideration of potential differences" (Whyte, 2015: 15, 2024) beyond abstraction. My anti-racist, anti-colonialist method of interpreting Leopoldian narratives, employing Whyte's "three issues that complicate any attempt to compare versions of Leopoldian and Indigenous ethics" (Whyte, 2015: 8, 2024), centers the expertise of those who are Indigenous and/or racialized as non-white, and all those on the frontlines of systemic oppression. It seeks to listen for understanding.

This method meshes with an intergenerational methodology of narrative criticism, which is informed by literary scholar Robert Pogue Harrison's *Dominion of the Dead* (2003). Looking to Leopold as my cultural ancestor, I retrieve Leopoldian narratives and reconsider what proposals, in whole or in part, to (1) avow, (2) refuse, and/or (3) rejoinder in the service of unraveling narratives of white supremacist settler colonialism and to challenge its custom of canonization itself. I intentionally apply this conversational methodology in order to prevent my work from becoming merely academic and unmoored from real relationships, including with the dead. The matrix of Indigenous-led method and intergenerationally responsible methodology, in generating unshrinking criticism as well as respect and care, helps guard against temptations to extremes, of ancestral hagiography or of cancelation. In either case, the troubles would be allowed to live on below the surface shaping current thinking (Harrison, 2003:102; Gilio-Whitaker, 2019: 94–95).

It is challenging to resist and revise one's internalized privilege and the powerful system that keeps propping it up. It requires intention and the reciprocal support of others. I hope that the repeated application of this matrix to key examples of Leopoldian narratives might be adaptable to other settler legacies, for instance, in helping form search images for normalized white supremacist, colonizing, and intersectionally domineering human power relations and in helping practice such searching habits of mind. Although I do not intend cancelation, I do propose intentionally diminished attention on Leopold's and other more or less known settler conservationist works, thus also my own modest contributions. I also encourage overall de-canonization that would continue allowing a few voices to overshadow more voices. I encourage privileging attention on hosts of too-often unheard works, particularly of those on the frontlines of oppression. This could include reading the works and following the literary trails of many cited through this Element, trails on which I also look forward to continuing.

I hope that this Element will help the settler wildlife scientist and educator, and the settler agrarian, who look up to Leopold as to a founder. I hope they can take courage to question even the validity of research based in erasures of Indigenous Peoples and to privilege Indigenous scientific expertise. I hope it can help the settler philosopher to rethink settler ethics within Indigenous-led collaborations and support the liberation of the Indigenous philosopher from settler-presumptions of Leopold's relevance; the English literary scholar to develop their own anti-colonialist praxis; the Chinese-language reader and poet admiring *A Sand County Almanac* to reconsider the imposition of this and other U.S. settler narratives on her culture; and the Ohkay Owingeh Pueblo matriarch and author to be among the last whose teachers have insensitively assigned Leopold's book as a model with no alternatives.

I propose that whenever *A Sand County Almanac* and other works by Leopold are read it be taken as opportunity: (1) to practice this Element's method and methodology, calling out, discussing, and organizing ways to refuse the white supremacist settler colonialism that weaves it; (2) to call in readers to critical study of historic, ongoing injurious influences, for example, in normalized assumptions, ontologies, movements, institutionalized policies, land use, and other relational practices and into needed deep revisioning along with the renewal of any still-avowable aspects; (3) to go forward open to hearing Indigenous refusals of we settlers – not everything is for us; and (4) to proceed practicing something like "a panacoustic politics" that integrates listening within sound strata (including the unhearable) and historical contexts in positionally responsible, self-reflexive, and co-creative ways (Robinson 2020: 59–60) in support of Land (Water, Language) Back and beyond any relational frameworks and so on that I could now imagine.

I hope, in these ways and others, that this Element, overall, will support settler realignment with "the collective genius of all the people who have survived these wicked systems," as the Dominican-American author Junot Díaz says (Tallbear, 2019: 34). Along these lines, as Tallbear says, "we can have radical hope in a narrative that entails not redeeming the state but caring for one another as relations" (34). To do so, she says, "we must strike blows whenever possible to the dominant narrative of a multicultural and supposedly progressive (always progressing toward greater good) settler state," which "misguides us in our 'genius' and in our ability to live with each other" (34–35). This includes dominant narratives of U.S. conservation; these include Leopoldian ones. We must make room on shelves, syllabi, and in priorities to release opportunities for arrays of liberatory geniuses to shine through.

I wish for this work to honor my teachers, including Native Movement's executive director Enei Begaye (Diné and Tohono O'odham, partnered with Neets'aii Gwich'in) and land protector and filmmaker Princess Daazhraii Johnson (Neets'aii Gwich'in). I wish this Element to support decolonization as they defined it early-on for me as:

> The conscious – intelligent, calculated, and active – unlearning and resistance to the forces of colonization that perpetuate the subjugation and exploitation

of our minds, bodies, and lands. And it is engaged for the ultimate purpose of overturning the colonial structure and realizing Indigenous liberation.[16]

Their instruction helped prepare me to receive that of others, also tied with abolitionist de/creative projects to undermine "race" as a taught system of practices (McClean, 2020) and to "undermine the [carceral] totalizing logics of empire, chattel, occupation, heteropatriarchy, racial-colonial genocide, and Civilization as a juridicial-narrative epoch" (Rodríguez, 2019: 1578). The instruction of my community helped prepare me to receive, of particular note for this Element, the works of Kyle Powys Whyte. Decolonization supports Indigenous "collective continuance," in Whyte's terms, the ongoingness of "ecologies" that co-create particular relational qualities, including responsibilities. The continuance of relationships, even more particularly than sovereignty, "refers to a society's capacity to self-determine how to adapt to change in ways that avoid reasonably preventable harms" (Whyte, 2018a: 131). Collective continuance occurs, in one way or another, beyond the U.S. (or any) settler-colonial state, which seeks the injustice of pre-empting others' ecologies with its own. A settler-colonial ecology – far from superior and exploitive as it is – is not even sustainable.

Leopoldian conservation narratives, while proposing "land health," the desired norm toward which Leopold's land ethic points, continue the unsustainable project of settler dominance. After reintroducing Leopold, further detailing this Element's method and methodology, and offering refusals of woven-in white supremacy based on it, including of my own rote repetitions, I bear witness – with consent, and as an invited participant-activist in three Alaska Native-led events. Deep listening for understanding is itself a rejoinder to Leopoldian dominance pointing toward Indigenous-led proposals for ethical and good relations and desired futures of "radical hope." These concluding episodes convey examples of Indigenous collective continuance in spite of U.S. settler-colonialism. They support the legibility of the ongoing existence of Indigenous Peoples, and reveal important differences between Leopoldian proposals for an ethical ecology and Gwich'in and other Indigenous perspectives on the way to decolonization.

1.1 Re-Introducing Aldo Leopold with Indigenous Land Acknowledgments

Aldo Leopold's parents were first cousins, both children of nineteenth-century U.S. immigrants from Germany. In 1887 Leopold was born in Burlington, Iowa. This city and state were founded by taking ancestral and historic lands upon

---

[16] www.nativemovement.org; As presented at Howard Luke Gaalee'ya Spirit Camp, Alaska Art-in-Action, 2018.

which many Indigenous Nations depended, including the Očhéthi Šakówiŋ (Lakota), and to which, in the eighteenth-century, the allied oθaakiiwaki·hina·ki (Sauk) & Meškwahki·aša·hina (Fox) had arrived after being forced from Eastern Woodland Culture areas to the north and east.[17] U.S. genocidal forces had disrupted Indigenous ecologies and societies to pave the way for European settlement barely a generation before Leopold's own forebears' arrived.

In 1909, Leopold graduated from the new Yale Forest School, occupying customary lands of several more Algonquin-speaking Peoples, including Mohegan and Peekwot. That same year, he began his career as a forest and game manager for the United States Forest Service in the U.S.-dominated and denominated Territories of Arizona and New Mexico. While these two would become new States in 1912, they are the countries of dozens of other First Nations, including tribes of Navajo, Apache, and many Pueblos. Each has their own history of prior centuries of Spanish colonization, of Mexican independence, and/or U.S. expansion, removals, and dismemberments. Near the southwestern forests where Leopold worked children and grandchildren of African slaves lived. One of the U.S. Army's segregated Black regiments, called "Buffalo Soldiers," were stationed to the south at Fort Huachuca, near the Arizona-Mexico border, entangled in border fights including against Apache and Pancho Villa (Savoy, 2016: 142–147). It was from within this geography that Leopold helped define the "wilderness idea" in the U.S. and establish the "Gila Wilderness Area," the first official wilderness in the U.S. forest system.

In 1924, Leopold moved his family to Madison, Wisconsin. Nine years later, his formative *Game Management* textbook was published and he was hired at the University of Wisconsin, where he taught until his death in 1948. Far longer than "Madison" had occupied the area, this geography has been homelands of the Hoocąk Nation and/or many others, including, the Očhéthi Šakówiŋ, the oθaakiiwaki·hina·ki & Meškwahki·aša·hina, the Kiikaapoi (Kickapoo), the Myaamia (Miami), and the nearby Bodwéwadmi (Potawatomi) and the Omāēqnomenew-ahkew (Menominee).[18] This is the

---

[17] These two Nations have a history of alliance predating the founding of the United States, also fending off French and other European colonizers and other Indigenous Tribes. The U.S., after slaughtering Sauk farmers in their (Illinois) homelands in 1832 (aka the "Black Hawk War"), "officially combined" the Nations as "Sac & Fox." In 1845, the U.S. removed them (though some stayed in Iowa) to a reservation in Kansas and stole their homelands. By purchasing thousands of acres of their homelands, however, these two still-allied tribes have retained sovereignty within their historic territory ("Meskwaki Nation, About Us: History," https://meskwakipowwow.com/meskwaki-history; www.meskwaki.org/about-us/; Dunbar-Ortiz, 2014: 111). Iowa Native American Council has a list of "Tribal Nations that had homelands in Iowa," https://nativeamericancouncil.org.uiowa.edu/acknowledgement-land-and-sovereignty.

[18] Native Land Digital, https://native-land.ca.

area within which Leopold conceived the book that became *A Sand County Almanac*.

In Part I of *A Sand County Almanac* – the culmination of his lifetime of work, published post-humously in 1949 – Leopold shared stories of personal land encounters between 1935 and the mid-1940s. These occurred as he with his family tried "to rebuild" (1949: viii) a worn-out settler-farm near Madison, in Baraboo, Wisconsin. In Part II, "Sketches Here and There," Leopold discussed ways the U.S. mainstream industrial-capitalist culture – from Lenapehoking Manhattan to Iizhik Gwats'an Gwandaii Goodlit the Artic Refuge's Coastal Plain (and beyond) – was "out of step" with a "conservation" focus. The geographical scope of the book broadened in this section, and the tone became more straightforwardly argumentative. In Part III, "The Upshot," Leopold presented a philosophical inquiry that links "the land ethic" and "land health" – presumably adaptable to any landscape – and, central to my own book, *Aldo Leopold's Odyssey*. Leopold most succinctly and famously defined the scientifically informed ethical "right" in land-use as that which "tends to preserve the integrity, stability, and beauty of the biotic community" (Leopold, 1949: 224).

At every step in his career, though not acknowledging it with the respect justice calls for, Leopold is treading on and writing about Native land.

1.2 Rescoping Personal Responsibility

But then the same is true of all of us white settlers. As I critique and rejoinder Leopold's writings, I do likewise to my own as author of *Aldo Leopold's Odyssey: Rediscovering the Author of* A Sand County Almanac. In my book, "odyssey" refers to the development of Leopold's scientific *and* normative concept of "land health," to which his famous "land ethic" points. It also references Leopold's essay "Odyssey," which portrays the "ecological odyssey" of life in a give-and-take of energy and chemicals intersecting with an "evolutionary odyssey" in a succession of life, organizing and complexifying, along a rolling arrow of time (2016: 12). I retain all of these senses of "odyssey" in this Element, adding in aspects of my own journey. I also stress how these three facets are encapsulated in my own book and are woven together with oppressive, including genocidal as well as eugenic, assumptions. For instance, woven with assumptions that Indigenous people, if human beings at all, are inferior ones compared with dominating norms, are already gone; or, inevitably and/or by design will soon disappear. Again, I am surfacing such grave narrative troubles, in detail, in order to refuse and rejoinder white supremacist settler colonialism. I do so in support of decolonization and of abolition, that is in support of deeply revisioned, intersectional, ontological, narrative, and structural change "defying a [mere] liberal-to-reactionary (white/multiculturalist) common sense" (Rodríguez, 2019: 1578), which would merely allow the simplistic, familiar, realistic, and/or ideological to trump what is necessary. This is what I mean by the verb "unsettling" in the title of my Element.

I have long been a student of Aldo Leopold's maturing ideas about land-human relationships. This is evident in the care I took writing my book. In both the 2006 and 2016 editions of *Odyssey*, however, I left out the above acknowledgments and much else. *Odyssey* was first written as my PhD dissertation after a ten-year span between degree programs. On *Aldo Leopold's Odyssey*'s tenth anniversary, it was republished under my new name, coming after my divorce and a new marriage, in a still ongoing journey to liberation. The divorce, occurring alongside my doctoral graduation, also involved alienation from the totalizing religious culture on which I had submissively imprinted for more than thirty years. My entire support system, like the first marriage, fell to pieces. This shattering had been precipitated by an all-too-familiar and ever-unique story – enmeshment with a man experienced at psychological and sexual grooming, a smart and, I thought, more progressive person and leading academic whom I had trusted as my advisor.[19] The personal and professional fragmentation, over time and involving much (ongoing) healing work, paradoxically, has turned out to include a gift of (also ongoing) release from my former untenable worldview at the intersection of religious fundamentalism and both U.S. conservative and liberal slants on heteropatriarchy.

I had and still have a lot to un/learn and worlds to re/orient to. My new Preface to the 2016 anniversary edition of *Aldo Leopold's Odyssey* highlighted aspects of Leopold's work made more salient by awareness of global climate change alongside "not only an industrialized, but an increasingly human-populated, class-divided, and urbanized planet" (xxi), as I then put it. And, relatedly, the provocative, best-selling climate change author and dynamic movement builder Bill McKibben, who was a Leopold admirer, generously contributed a Foreword. Leopold, McKibben said, "was clearly interested in wilderness." At the same time, McKibben emphasized that Leopold's "land health" ideal, the focus of my book, "was a quieter vision of the world, and perhaps a more radical one" than his interest in wilderness indicated. Leopold, did, after all, come to recognize, McKibben notes, that "there was no way to wall man off from the rest of the world" (Warren, 2016: xi).

Leopold saw his own ethical work as a radical pursuit – to "the roots of the problem" (Leopold, 1993: 157) – of a conservation, culminating in land health,

---

[19] This is *not* the same person who saw me through to the end of my degree and signed off on my dissertation.

that involved doctoring (Callicott and Freyfogle, 1999: 220; see also Leopold, 1933: 411; Flader and Callicott, 1991: 288) an "environmental fracture," a conceptual division of "man" and "nature," in the terms of the Caribbean political philosopher Malcolm Ferdinand. Leopold was working out this sort of mending, however, merely *within* his and my own culture's extractive worldview, which encompassed ongoing utilitarian forms of U.S. conservation that severed nature into parts, caste away some parts as useless while profiting from others deemed "resources," and educated students' intellects without nurturing affection for land.

Throughout his career, Leopold tried out various angles in pursuit of solving root problems, preferring positive or constructive ones (e.g., Flader and Callicott, 1991: 345), both in his writing and as an organizer and educator. For instance, in the 1910s, Leopold, serving in USFS District 3, was put in charge of coordinating a new fish and game program. He did award-winning work, traveling across his region of the Southwest supporting the organization of new game protective associations with the ideal to "restore to every citizen his inalienable right to know and love wild things of his native land" (Warren, 2016: 87). While serving for a short time as secretary of the Albuquerque Chamber of Commerce, Leopold organized a city tree-planting campaign. He hoped it would not only restore appropriate plants to the community but help unite factions problematic, he thought, to achieving a common cause of a good place to live. Later, in Wisconsin, Leopold incentivized "Coon Valley" farmers as private landowners to work for the "mutually advantageous" public interest in land use (Callicott and Freyfogle, 1999: 164; Lin, 2014; Warren, 2016: 155). As he came to the final year of his life, Leopold became one of several founding advisors to the Conservation Foundation, an organization intending to promote "worldwide democratice peace and ecological conservation" (Warren, 2016: xxi). Leopold leaned away from "direct agitation," though, as the group agreed that their purpose was to "maintain dignity and high professional integrity" and bring "underlying truth" into conservation education and into "objective fact-finding" research (xxvii).

Education and research, woven with the "ethos" of rhetorics or the "persona" of literature, remain potent tools for persuasion if not transformation, to be sure (Cryer, 2015). And, repeatedly, as we shall see, Leopold returned to a growing conviction that what was needed to bring about his land ethical ideas, at the root of roots, was an internal change in people bringing about an "ecological conscience." Yet dignity in professionalism often translated into approaches of a certain practical caution, or "liberal-to-reactionary (white/multiculturalist) common sense" in Rodríguez's terms, where acts of advocacy were concerned. Such caution can be a symptom of Euro-settler comfort. This is a racialized privilege, for instance, that would allow Leopold to address *A Sand County Almanac* to the homogenized "us" who were, by "mechanization," "assured . . . of a good breakfast," and who could afford "a little healthy contempt for a plethora of material blessings" (1949: ix); this is the privilege that allowed the assumption that "a shift of values" was needed and not liberation from landlessness due to theft "when we took [land] over from the Indians," continent-wide (Callicott and Freyfogle, 1999: 162); this is the privilege that allowed his "we" to erase ongoing condonation of enslavement – of a profit-driven ethic in using people and land – in imaging that this "philosophy is dead in human relations"; this is the privilege that allowed assuming there is no other "we" than the one who has already taken "19 centuries to define decent man-to-man conduct" (albeit "only half done") and through whom "it may take as long to evolve a code of decency for man-to-land conduct" (Flader and Callicott, 345–6; see also Leopold, 1993: 155). This is the particular "we" who might evolve sooner in sympathy with eugenics in multiple guises encouraging, for instance, those with a "racial inheritance" of "an interest in wildlife" (Leopold, et al., 1937: 26) as earth's inheritors.

As I argue throughout this Element, neither Leopold nor I have been nearly radical enough or altogether not radical, when it comes to seeing and resisting white supremacist settler-colonialism woven through our own perspectives on land and people relations. Leopoldian works maintain a "colonial fracture," in Ferdinand's terms, sustained by Eurocentric racism and imperialism, that makes hierarchical separations between "European colonizers and non-European colonized peoples, between Whites and non-Whites, between the masters and the enslaved, between the metropole and the colonies, between the Global North and the Global South" (2022: 4–7). And, Leopoldian narratives – from the beginning to the end of his career – maintain such structured power relations without recognizing that rooting out assumptions that some people will dominate others goes hand in hand with tending human-land relationships. And this gives pause to acknowledge that the environmental fracture became actionably salient to him, me, and many other U.S. settler conservationists when the colonial one did not. Perhaps this is because, demanding as it might be to shift settler land values, it can seem less threatening and more appealing than unsettling them.

Meanwhile, initiated by advice from his daughter, McKibben says, he prioritized leveraging his culturally privileged standing and global platform. Not responding defensively, his actions have included transitioning in July 2020 to "emeritus status" in 350.org, an influential climate organization which he co-founded, "to lower the volume" on his own influence while remaining supportive, particularly of rising generations of leadership. As, around this time, he also founded TH!RD ACT to organize aging climate justice activists to address ongoing intergenerational troubles wherein "inclusive" sounds attached to a theory of structural justice. Their principles include, for instance, that "differences of race, gender, or other markers of identity make us stronger" and that "everyone has a role" in undoing "unjust and unhealthy" societal patterns.[20] McKibben began practicing not hoarding attention and "passing the mic" to those who – with their communities – are often most hazarded yet least heard by those doing the climate warming, including Native, Black and Brown persons, especially who also are women, youth, and/or LGBTQIA+, and/or disabled persons (McKibben, 2022).[21] The host of important voices to whom he has drawn attention have included Mary Annaïse Heglar and Bernadette Demientieff. Heglar is a Black woman speaking broadly as a "Public Climate Person," in her words.[22] While a writer-in-residence at Columbia University's Earth Institute, her challenging reflections hit home to me as I, too, had been a New Yorker living through Superstorm Sandy. I taught on the New York University faculty during the 2012 storm, which certainly laid bare worlds of inequities. This included students I knew.[23] This, and the wider situation – people already in intersectionally precarious living situations now also facing transportation shutdowns, electricity outages and an unsafe water supply, uninhabitable homes, and other catastrophic storm losses – broke through a buffer of my own privileges.

Climate stressors rise from and magnify the injustices, oppression, and griefs perpetuated by white supremacy.[24] This includes racialized non-white students assigned "staple texts" like Leopold's *Almanac*, to find their lived experiences

---

[20] *Third Act*, https://thirdact.org/about/working-principles/; In his recent *The Flag, The Cross, and The Station Wagon* (2022), McKibben, a white, cis-male settler, acknowledges how lives like his were built "on the suffering of others" (54); is enlarging on earlier generations of normalized U.S. history education, (finally) coming to "enslaved people and Native people . . . .as main characters" and as speaking for themselves; is pausing while considering what might be salvageable from his former (and racist) understandings and "what reparations we must make" before re-telling old stories in ways that may be (at least) "a little revolutionary again" (28), which, I gander, is to become altogether radical.

[21] Also McKibben, B. (2020). "A Letter to My Colleagues at 350.org," https://350.org/bill-mckibbens-letter/; McKibben, B. (2020). "The most important thing: Interview by Maria Virginia Olano," https://climate-xchange.org/2020/05/15/bill-mckibben-interview/; McKibben, B. (2020). "A Bomb in the Middle of the Climate Movement," www.rollingstone.com/politics/political-commentary/bill-mckibben-climate-movement-michael-moore-993073/.

[22] Heglar M.A. (2020). We Can't Tackle Climate Change Without You, www.wired.com/story/what-you-can-do-solve-climate-change.

[23] Warren, J. (2021). "Connecting the Dots," https://humansandnature.org/connecting-the-dots-occupy-times-square-unsettle-imaginations-2021/.

[24] Burton, N. (2020). "People of Color Experience Grief More Deeply Than White People," www.vice.com/en_us/article/v7ggqx/people-of-color-experience-climate-grief-more-deeply-than-white-people; Nieves, et al. (2020). "There Is No Climate Justice Without Racial Justice," www.yesmagazine.org/environment/2020/06/12/climate-justice-racial-justice.

and interests "left in the dust" (Savoy, 2015: 33–34).[25] It includes criminalization of non-white people outdoors, as in the infamous Central Park birding incident – Christian Cooper, a Black man, was birdwatching when a white woman, feeling threatened by his very presence, called the police on him.[26] In 2020, reflecting on Sandy's lessons, Heglar reiterated how climate science supports "the severity of the injustice" – that is, those contributing to climate change the least tend to suffer the most. "Sure," she says, "but it's not the entire story." How will various sectors – educational, recreational, economic – lean into what sciences help point to? There's a place, scientist or not, Heglar explains, for anyone who "understands the concept of 'no fair.'" This "no fair," as she stresses, includes understanding climate – really, everything connecting to land and to health – as "the Black issue it is."[27]

Heglar's "no fair" is also the Indigenous issue. I left New York, occupying Lenapehoking, for the city of Fairbanks, Alaska, on unceded ancestral lands of the lower Tanana Dene Peoples. This is where I first met Bernadette Demientieff, Gwich'yaa Zhee Gwich'in and Director of the Gwich'in Steering Committee. As noted in Section 1, the Introduction, the Committee was formed within her Nation in 1988 for defending Iizhik Gwats'an Gwandaii Goodlit The Sacred Place Where Life Begins (in U.S. political terms, the Arctic National Wildlife Refuge Coastal Plain 1002 Area) against oil and gas drilling threats and for educating non-Gwich'in on their reasons to protect it. Demientieff stresses what defending this sacred land means for her: "This is not just about a wilderness," she says. "Of course we are all interconnected up here to our land, water, and animals. And, if our animals and our land is sick then we are sick."[28] Conveying her Elders' message, Demientieff emphasizes that she is "not an environmentalist or activist." She is Gwich'in, and this "is not just about protecting our polar bears but this is about Indigenous voices being

---

[25] Gatheru, W. (2020). "It's Time for Environmental Studies to Own Up to Erasing Black People," www.vice.com/en/article/889qxx/its-time-for-environmental-studies-to-own-up-to-erasing-black-people; see also Jones, R. (2020). "The Environmental Movement Is Very White," www.nationalgeographic.com/history/2020/07/environmental-movement-very-white-these-leaders-want-change-that/.

[26] Betancourt, D. (2020). "Christian Cooper Hopes," www.washingtonpost.com/arts-entertainment/2020/06/23/christian-cooper-central-park-birder-comics/; Lanham, D. (2018). "Forever Gone," https://orionmagazine.org/article/forever-gone.

[27] Heglar, M.A. (2020). "We Don't Have to Halt Climate Action to Fight Racism," www.huffpost.com/entry/climate-crisis-racism-environmenal-justice_n_5ee072b9c5b6b9cbc7699c3d; "How Can We Build a Hardier World After the Coronavirus," www.newyorker.com/news/annals-of-a-warming-planet/how-we-can-build-a-hardier-world-after-the-coronavirus; We Can't Tackle Climate Change Without You, www.wired.com/story/what-you-can-do-solve-climate-change/.

[28] Demientieff, B. (2020). Rothko Chapel Oscar Romero Award Ceremony, https://vimeo.com/136731614.

ignored, this is about a whole identity, about a people's entire way of life being destroyed for profit."[29]

In *Aldo Leopold's Odyssey*, I developed Leopold's critiques of dominating, harmful, profit-driven, industrial-capitalist land relationships. He evaluated such relations not only as imprudent but also as ethically "wrong." As a rejoinder, he offered a positive narrative of a necessary transition to "right" and healthful human-land relationships. This narrative, still considered radical or visionary, or at least crucial, by numbers of scholars and/or conservationists, was based in evolutionary and ecological science. Furthermore, Leopold's evidence-based knowledge was entwined with "love and respect" for self-organizing, regenerative communities of soils, waters, air, plants, and animals, including humans, at least some of us. In *Aldo Leopold's Odyssey*, I went to great lengths to detail how Leopold, characteristically teachable and curious, both refused or otherwise unlearned some settler-conventional ways to imagine land and learned some new ways to see it. In this regard, for example, he shifted from participation in U.S. wolf-elimination projects to supporting their rightful and functional membership within the land community, if not on equal footing with learned conservationists as intelligent teachers themselves and beings to be thanked (Simpson, 2014; Fix et al., 2019; Van Horn, et al., 2021). The "biotic pyramid" symbol Leopold helped detail replaces what he deemed a less-apt balancing scale image. His proposed "mental image" portrays land as a "fountain of energy flowing through a circuit of soils, plants, and animals," albeit wherein "Indians" were replaced by "farmers," as superior human animals. Moreover, "wilderness," Leopold claimed, was the "most perfect norm" by which to evaluate the healthy functioning of a human-inhabited land's "biotic pyramid." Wilderness protection, Leopold also argued, should be a common ground for scientists and recreationalists at odds on other points within settler-colonial society (Warren, 2008).

"Wilderness," written conceptually and politically on the ground, is a known site of racialized danger and relational disruptions as so many persons continue expounding (Merchant, 1989; Denevan,1992; Cronon, 1996; Catton, 1997; Spence 1999; Nelson and Callicott, 2008; Whyte, 2018a; Gomez et al., 2018; Ferdinand, 2022; Sharkey, 2023; Dawson et al., 2023).[30] Wilderness is a place where Black persons continue to be vulnerable to violence by white persons. It

---

[29] Demientieff, B. (2020). "What Will It Take to Cool The Planet?: Pass the Mic: Interview by Bill McKibben," www.newyorker.com/news/annals-of-a-warming-planet/what-will-it-take-to-cool-the-planet; Warren, 2024.

[30] Gilio-Whitaker, D. (2020). "The Problem with Wilderness," www.uuworld.org/articles/problem-wilderness ; Gilio-Whitaker, D. (2022), "Environmental Justice," www.hcn.org/issues/54.7/indigenous-affairs-perspective-environmental-justice-is-only-the-beginning; IMAGO Initiative. (2023). "Reimagining Conservation Through an Indigenous Lens," The Wilderness Society at www.wilder

is an ongoing act of boundary-making with rippling consequences to Lands' Native Peoples, disrupting customary and historic ecologies and threatening collective continuance. As a concept by and for largely able-bodied Euro-colonizers, "wilderness" cancels the all-too-real and still-unfolding histories of the U.S. government's murderous and otherwise forcible removals and assimilations of Indigenous people to appropriate their homelands.

This colonialist activity engaged Leopold's first employer, the United States Forest Service, and Leopold himself. Leopold did encompass human beings in his ecological-ethical concept of land health. Referring to wilderness as its best comparative norm, however, is only one of the ways in which his ideas of land community membership were exclusive. It is important to repeat that Leopold's works expressing intentions to repair a human-land fracture not only do not themselves represent nor inherently translate into just, anti-racist, decolonial, and/or abolitionist relational mending. As we shall see in further detail, his narratives are woven with colonialist white supremacy and attendant structures of authority. Thus, subsequent well-meaning efforts at diversity and inclusivity, for instance, by the Aldo Leopold Foundation, The Land Institute, The Society for Conservation Biology, the IUCN, in policies like the U.S. Wilderness Act, or in books like my *Aldo Leopold's Odyssey* and *Last Great Wilderness* by Roger Kaye, and any other small to vast institutions, movements, policies, writings, research, or agendas attached to Leopoldian norms – without tending the colonial fracture still throbbing within them – unfortunately, would be prone to reinscribe their offenses.

It follows that it is crucial to continue alert so as not to mistake the adaptation of a colonialist word, scheme, and/or legal tool for the most apt tool for environmental justice and rightful Indigenous access to sacred sites. For instance, the Gwich'in Nation's resolution, Gwich'in Niinstyaa, calls on the U.S. government to designate the so-called 1002 area of the Arctic Refuge a "Wilderness" in order to protect the Porcupine Caribou calving grounds, "for generations to come," land that will never stop being Iizhik Gwats'an Gwandaii Goodlit The Sacred Place Where Life Begins.[31] "Wilderness" may be the best available of "sites of interaction," in Whyte's terms, (2014: 3) – if not a conceptual, a political sphere the Gwich'in find of use against the threat of big oil extraction. Yet, any policy not incorporating "Indigenous conceptions of relationality," as Gilio-Whitaker discusses, "will ultimately reproduce relationships of [colonialist] domination" (2019: 145; Warren, 2024). Addressing those interested in "continental scale

---

ness.org/key-issues/wildlands-everyone/imago-initiative; Sené-Harper, A. (2022). "Land Grabs and Conservation Propaganda," https://africasacountry.com/author/aby-l-sene.

[31] The Gwich'in Nation. (2022). Gwich'in Niintsyaa," https://trustees.org/wp-content/uploads/2022/07/RES-Gwichin-Niintsyaa_PASSED_22Jul19.pdf.

conservation," Neets'aii Gwich'in Elder, Doctor, and Reverend Trimble Gilbert, for instance, "reminds us that before his homeland was overlain with the Western refuge-wilderness-conservation ideology," the Gwich'in have had their own successful relationships and place-based worldview that "underpins the Gwich'in peoples' strident efforts to protect the Refuge's coastal plain as Wilderness, and their expanding advocacy for just and sustainable environmental policies" (Kaye et al., 2021; Warren, 2024).

At an expandingly global scale, Leopold himself and we who have followed in his footsteps might find ourselves thinking we substantially agree with the 2021 "Marseille Manifesto: A People's Manifesto for the Future of Conservation," co-created by many Indigenous and non-Indigenous activists and experts worldwide. It calls out "a model of conservation" that Leopold also worked against, one contributing to rather than thwarting biodiversity loss due to "the rampant expansion of a growth-oriented industrial economy" valuing land and its life as capital. How many Leopoldian conservationists, though, are working for a "complete halt in the creation of new Protected Areas, which exclude Indigenous and local communities," including in U.S. wilderness policies? How many of us refuse to embark "on any conservation projects without the full Free, Prior, and Informed Consent (FPIC) of the communities concerned"? How many know proper protocol for and prioritize "concrete plans for reparations of past wrongs, including through transferring control back to the historical and local guardians"? (Dawson, et al., 2023: 229). And how many shall continue responsibly listening for how expressions of extinction, climate, and any other land-based crisis, "like every contemporary crisis, has more to do with justice, with structural violence and racism, with land theft, and with colonialism than with what we, in the Global North call 'environment,' 'climate,' and 'nature'"? (Longo in Dawson, et al., 2023: 7).

In both editions of *Aldo Leopold's Odyssey*, as I have begun to see, I represented white settler-colonialist ontologies and repeated histories that hide atrocities and suppress and disrupt Indigenous knowledges and ecologies. By such complicitous repetitions I helped perpetuate a legacy of violent actions in the present. This story, not unique to me, illustrates how critiquing for-profit capitalism (or commodifying socialism, for that matter) in land valuations, as important as it is, is not enough. Acts of surfacing deep structures of power relations are needed to reveal the linkages of even the most well-meaning ventures – including within conservation, including within Leopoldian narratives – with U.S. white supremacist settler-colonialism – its genocides, forced assimilations, land thefts, and essential slave labor (Warren, 2016: 171, 443fn85; Demuth, 2019).

I concluded *Aldo Leopold's Odyssey* as a history of transformational conservation work begun by Leopold but left undone at his death. For me, at the time, land health was the dynamic ideal to which his land ethic pointed along with so many challenges ahead to enact it. Between 2006 and 2016, as I note in the Preface to the Tenth Anniversary Edition, I felt all the more clearly how shifting contexts and new understandings must alter my own work as well. Throughout that decade I had become deeply engaged, via 350.org and the broadening fossil fuel divestment movement, in intergenerational community organizing for system change. As a faculty member, this had meant becoming a better listener to youth, and for several years I was active in co-constituting my relations with students, both in classrooms and in climate justice actions. That decade's experiences had also made different points in Leopold's works salient to me. For example, in that 2016 Preface, it seemed important to note Leopold's historic advisory role in launching the Conservation Foundation, because they later convened one of the earliest conferences on anthropogenic climate change. Leopold's insight, during a world war, that "many conservation problems heretofore local will shortly become global," appeared all the more relevant in the twenty-first century (Warren, 2016: xxiv). I was compelled to explore how Leopold's ecological concept of land – the land health focus of *Odyssey* – might remain germane, since it was not only temporally dynamic but also "spatially elastic." His "biotic pyramid" was ever-expansionary in this emerging view. It linked naturally from local to world-wide scales and from fossil hydrocarbons underground to soils and industrial emissions of global atmospheric carbon bringing on global warming (xxx–xxxiv). Nowhere, even in this later edition, did I directly locate and face menacing projections of exclusionary white supremacy and ecologies-laminating settler colonialism, including within Leopoldian narratives.

There are signs that I searched for indications that Leopold might have become increasingly concerned about oppressed people, if not seeing the intersection of conservation troubles with colonial structures, and justice. For instance, I noted that Leopold had penciled in "Labor Unions" as another potential group to enlist in possible political action in the margin of a Conservation Foundation discussion document alongside "rotary, 4-H, Boy Scouts, chambers of commerce, and women's federations" (xxvii). In this document, which framed the organization's educational- and research-based purpose, I was sure to list some of their "fact-finding" interests, including the "protection needs of endangered fauna, flora, wilderness of varying degrees, and indigenous people" (xxviii). These interests not only did not speak to justice and respect but remain offensively objectifying, dehumanizing, and patronizing. Nor did I note that Leopold was directly supportive of the works of other

Foundation associates, such as conservationist authors Bill Vogt and Henry Fairfield Osborn, Jr., who were more outspoken in making Malthusian and/or eugenic proposals. The closest I got to linking environmental and colonial fractures was probably in recognizing that those "least responsible for escalating troubles" (xxxv) were suffering first and most.

Along similar lines, I made my own apparently subconscious moves to innocence (Tuck and Yang, 2012), on behalf of my cultural ancestor, Leopold, and myself. For instance, I am alarmed to see that, in joining quotes from two sources, I made it sound as if Leopold was not only noticing but also encouraging "people of 'suppressed' traditions" to "*'throw your weight around'*" in conservation matters. This smacks of my own white arrogance, presumption, and privilege (Warren, 2016: xxvii). Additionally, I preempted what Leopold actually had written in his unpublished draft titled "Ecology as an Ethical System."[32] "Other races, now suppressed," he had said, "might have somewhat different behavior patterns" than those of "the races now dominant." I had replaced Leopold's word "race" with "tradition." This switch of guises revealed my own discomfort with facing the underlying terms of inequitable power relations. It pointed to my uneasiness at the vexing implications of a sweeping proposal that the conservation profession be about changing land-ruining people into land ethical ones (see also, e.g., Flader and Callicott, 1991: 280). It avoided raising questions about who needed to change (or not) and how. His attempt in this draft to reckon, in historic and evolutionary time scales, with mutable or immutable human social components and variations in races that were dominant or suppressed while proposing the role of conservation as "routing the world's traffic," remained incomplete and confusing. Yet I had bypassed an overall framing that leaned toward more overtly popular eugenics (Prum, 2017), with which he too engaged, as well as Malthusian population control. These tendencies, too, need unearthing in order to refuse re-inventing their oppressions.

To draw out one more example of my complicity, I made a particularly glaring reprise of harmful arrogance in the conclusion to the 2016 Preface of *Aldo Leopold's Odyssey*. In the 1940s, Leopold had called for a "new kind of [land-health-minded] people"[33] Uncritically, I followed his example to propose "a new name for this offshoot of our own evolving species: *Homo generativus*" followed by a presumptuous, homogenizing, assimilative "We" (Warren, 2016: xxxv). Along with more cringe-worthy hubris, implicit in that sentence is the ongoing erasures of distinct, ancient and still-living Indigenous Peoples, from

---

[32] ca.1940s, LP 10-6, 17(4): 900-01.
[33] Leopold. (October 23, 1944). Letter to Douglas Wade, LP 9/25/10-8, 1(3): 465.

whom lands have been stolen, and Black and Brown people, stolen from homelands worldwide. Yet more. In my academic training and in my own academic work, I have learned and propagated the institutionalized erasures of these erasures in settler-colonial storytelling. Meanwhile, many Indigenous cultures have long proven what to Leopold and I remained merely wishful thinking, that "they have no need of the word 'conservation'" because they already "have the thing itself" (Callicott and Freyfogle, 1999: 172). Nor, it seems, do all systems and all Peoples require transformation so much as liberation.

I am responsible for doing better. My doing better means learning first how to listen (and how not to listen, i.e., extractively). My doing better includes commitments to go yet deeper and wider into my birth-culture's dominating – and routinely buried – rooted white supremacist and colonialist assumptions.[34] Oppressive assumptions of one-way authority have long structured relationships bearing injustice while undermining conditions of health and flourishing. Many remain still potently embedded in U.S. conservation, including its Leopoldian legacies. Still, Heglar holds space for anyone in the climate movement who "understands the concept of 'no fair.'" Demientieff is likewise generous: "we [Gwich'in] don't only think about … our people," she says, but also of "our human race" and "the many American people who deserve a chance at survival."[35] However, to leave out Heglar's summons to see climate as "the Black issue it is" and Demientieff's mustering non-Gwich'in to "stand with the Gwich'in Nation," and not the other way around, would be to *not* hear them.

2 Matrix of Methodology and Method

Bernadette Demientieff's elders call her to "to go out and tell the world that we are here." They say, "Do it in a good way," and "That 'do it in a good way,'" she acknowledges, "that is a very simple sentence, but it's not always easy, especially when we are up against so much dishonesty and misleading statements from our own [U.S.] government."[36] To learn about and stand with the Gwich'in Nation as they call for, however, I need to have a conversation with my own cultural elders and ancestors who have stood against hers. At the same time, I want to do this with care.

---

[34] Gilio-Whitaker, D. (2022). "Environmental Justice Is Only the Beginning," www.hcn.org/issues/54.7/indigenous-affairs-perspective-environmental-justice-is-only-the-beginning.
[35] Demientieff, B. (2020). Rothko Chapel Oscar Romero Award Ceremony, https://vimeo.com/136731614.
[36] Ibid.

2.1 Methodology: Good Conversations with Ancestors

At a glance, it might seem a faster route to reparative justice, abolitionist and decolonial futures to turn the white supremacist settler-colonial eraser around on my work and that of my forebears, including Leopold's.[37] Yet, as Robert Pogue Harrison brings to life in his *Dominion of the Dead,* deleting our culture-bearers could no more be done than canceling our birth parents. Each of us is layered with some heritage/s of shared assumptions and values that also define any norms of "virtue" and organize social institutions, including the institutions of conservation (Harrison, 2003: ix; Gilio-Whitaker, 2019: 92–95). What else could explain our existences, whether we acknowledge ourselves and ancestors or not?[38] And how, other than owning offences, can any of us reckon and do better?

Only in rare cases might a person or heritage be so abusive as to not have some brightness, including ourselves as human beings who wish to live on. At the moment our wish occurs, so does the certainty of our eventual death. As much as we might try to delay that certainty, the return to the company of our dead is inevitable. We can hardly escape them. But this does not necessarily lock rising generations into rote repetition of ancestral proposals. On the contrary, by facing them and disrupting our own willful ignorance, rising generations can make choices. By learning how to listen on the way to understanding, a way of respect, we can choose with care. Otherwise, we walk down a one-way street of hagiography or narcissistic authority – dead to living, elder to younger, colonizer to colonized, human to more-than-human. Driven on this way – perhaps like the insatiable monster Windigo whom mother, scientist-educator, author, and enrolled Citizen Potawatomi Nation Robin Wall Kimmerer describes in her Anishinaabe tradition (2013: 303–309) – deadends in the abuses of dominance. Listeners, however, can hear into the rapaciousness many settler predecessors have preferred to keep hidden. This includes the wide-reaching logics of "settler-native-slave triad" that erases its own tracks while leaving structures intact that erode land and violently eliminate Black and Native Peoples (Tuck and Yang, 2012: 18; Dotson, 2018: 195). Listeners can bring the secreted up to the surface – within U.S. conservation and in other environmental and social arenas – and thus un/learn and take responsibility.

---

[37] See, for example, on John Muir: Sahgún, L. (2014). "John Muir's Legacy Questioned," www.latimes.com/local/california/la-me-rethinking-muir-20141113-story.html. For ongoing discussion see John Muir Global Network, "Sierra Club vs. John Muir," https://johnmuir.org/sierra-club-vs-john-muir/.

[38] In a brutal irony, Alaska Natives in communities where racist colonizers have punished them for fidelity to their ancestral cultures, suicide is 3.5 times higher than the U.S. national average (Native Movement, et al. (2017). *We Breathe Again,* www.nativemovement.org/we-breathe-again-film).

2.1.1 To Listen and Respond: Dis/Avowals and Reciprocative Rejoinders

Harrison gleans insights from within an ancient to modern, secular Western legacy that might help some of its cultural descendants into an intergenerational methodology for becoming better living relations, and, eventually, ancestors.[39] Through "intercourse with the dead that is frank and ongoing with the past," in Harrison's words, some may move toward understanding what our predecessors are saying (Harrison, 2003: 102). To the degree that listeners hear and understand, we can flex responsible agency. We may, that is, discerningly say "yes" or "no" or "wait, I don't know" (yet?) to repeating the pasts' offerings. We may decide to refuse an old proposal outright, in whole or in part. We may decide to avow an antique pattern and practice it by rote, or we may update and renew it. In a third response, listeners may reciprocate with our ancestors by suggesting possible alternatives in the wake of refusals, filling imaginative voids with fresh options. In Harrison's terms, we may offer and/or support others' alternative proposals as "reciprocative rejoinders" to unwanted schemes, answering both coercive ancestors and those "who seek to make the historical present conform to an 'outstripped' past" (102). This conversational mode with the dead holds space and time for the living. Many Leopoldian followers, including myself, care deeply for him, his family and legacy. This conversational mode, by keeping things personal, also helps keep ourselves accountable (to ourselves). Whenever possible, it seems better to renew helpful and/or refuse harmful proposals – in this case, mainly narratives – of persons, not the persons themselves. In the present, the living may perceive multiple pasts and multiple futures in new ways. Counter to one-way authority, our perceptions hold open the possibility for complex, geographically particular reciprocities that produce echoing consequences across generations.

2.1.2 Paradox: Avowals Leading to Refusals

It is worth reminding ourselves that the fates of ancestors continually have yet to be decided by the descendants. "The old teachings," Kimmerer highlights, "recognized that Windigo nature is in each of us ... that we might learn why we should recoil from the greedy part of ourselves" (2013: 306; Langston, 2017). This applies to the institutions reifying greed. Reflecting on this might

---

[39] Harrison's work has been generative to think with, including some points with which I take issue."To be human means above all to bury," Harrison says (xi). Yet I wonder about his need to distinguish humans beings (and in universal ways) from other animals, in the first place. And I think it is a mistake to consider burial and/or awareness of death (perceiving a past and a future) as unique to human beings, not to mention human varieties of perspectives on time (ix, 34). Harrison also noncritically passes over stories of Euroamerican culture that pass over erasures of Indigenous Peoples (42).

also support giving consideration to others that we as individuals and communities would like to receive, *perhaps* even in our most ardent refusals. Adding to the complexities of the living-dead conversational framework are paradoxes wherein ancestors' unacceptable, even egregious attitudes and behaviors flow in and out of acceptable, even excellent ones. I hear this paradox, too, in returning, now again, to Leopold's legacy in the U.S. conservation movement as a still-powerful force both maintaining its heritage of institutions and policies and perhaps in change-making possibility.

My work here is primarily an intergenerational, conversational, critical assessment of extant, mostly canonized Leopoldian narratives supported by correspondences and other archival materials. At the same time, Leopold's words often emerged via interchanges with land-use projects, practicing would-be norms and models (Warren, 2016: xxix, 65, 266–289, 306–311, 395 fn 111). Other scholars have similarly pointed out that Leopold, like other nature writers before him, cast himself as a sort of "behavioral model" (Whyte, 2024; Cryer, 2015: 489). Keeping this in mind, I will look at three examples of Leopoldian proposals, in word and/or deed, that I still consider avowable, even excellent and that seem particularly generative: (1) intergenerational respect in disagreements between, for example, teacher and student; (2) intellectual humility or teachability (the willing capacity both to unlearn destructive land uses and to learn harmonious ones); and (3) solidarity, for instance, between conservationists with different priorities (e.g., hunting, birding, sustained forest harvest) for interconnected good. I renew these three proposals in the remaining parts of this section on the "Matrix of Methodology and Method," paradoxically, as a pathway to respectfully refuse the hegemonic white supremacy and settler-colonialism still woven into Leopold's conceptions. Concluding this section, then, my third avowal of solidarity moves into a disavowal of hegemony, overall, and my conversational methodology, informed by Harrison, meshes with my method of anti-colonialist review informed by the "three serious issues that must be reckoned with," raised by Whyte, in any comparisons of Leopoldian and North American Indigenous ethics (2015: 2, 2024).

Following this, Section 3 will explore each of Whyte's issues of reckoning, which I summarize here as: (1) unsound Leopoldian history-telling counter to many Indigenous narratives; (2) Leopoldian ethical abstractions with enactments counter to many Indigenous values; and (3) epistemological privileging of Western "systems of knowledge production" (10) normalized in or by Leopoldian narratives that suppress those of Indigenous Peoples and more marginalized by racializing white supremacy and settler-colonialism. Following Section 4, in which I turn the diagnostic lens back on my own Leopldian work, Section 5 listens to Alaska Native narratives. I propose settlers learning how to listen (to understand) and attunement with these and other Indigenous-led ventures, with openness to *not* know (Whyte, 2024; Robinson, 2020), as a possible reciprocative rejoinder, in the sense of my Harrison-based methodology, to Leopoldian dominance and in support of stabilizations of coalitions of settlers and Indigenous Peoples and more on the frontlines of oppression who may be working toward a common interest in habitable homes in a habitable Earth.

2.1.3 Avowing Intergenerational Respect to Refuse Settler-Colonialism

In *Aldo Leopold's Odyssey*, I include a story of Leopold's changing relationship with an early-career mentor. I repeat this story here in order to show respect for Leopold as one of my own most important early-career guides. By telling this story, I retrieve and avow Leopold's proposal of respect in disagreement – that is, a model of decent, compassionate, non-violent disagreement with one's own mentor. Renewing this in turn helps me, paradoxically, likewise, to retrieve and disavow other Leopoldian proposals.

William T. Hornaday's works loomed large for Leopold as a young supervisor in the United States Forest Service (USFS). In 1915, Leopold was assigned oversight of the USFS work on game and fish conservation in District 3 of the American Southwest. Hornaday's *Our Vanishing Wild Life* (1913) stoked Leopold's passions. Responsively, he organized local and state "game protective associations" (aka "GPAs") throughout the new U.S. states of Arizona and New Mexico, gaining national recognition. (Warren, 2016: 86–88). Conveying his mentor's influences, Leopold also wrote the first USFS *Game and Fish Handbook*. In this 1915 monograph, Leopold imitated Hornaday's words and combative tone. "If it is a crime to steal $25," Leopold wrote, "what shall we say of the extermination of a valuable species?" (Warren, 2016: 94). This kind of statement led me to assert, in *Aldo Leopold's Odyssey*, that "Leopold would remain firm in his belief in the goodness of life and in the wisdom of protecting it" (94). He did not change on this point. But I also discussed how Leopold parted ways with Hornaday "on the best means of protecting wildlife" (94). He altered his views. To their intergenerationally shared concern over threatened fauna, Leopold brought a fresh iteration of innovation, research, education, and authorship to the emerging profession of scientific forest management.

Hornaday's protectionist view had been popular for much of the previous generation. His writings recommended captive propagation, predator control (e.g., killing wolves and hawks), and limiting or banning hunting in new areas of "refuge." By the 1920s, various scientific conservationists were grumbling about other causes of population declines, mainly shrinking habitat, and the need to address them. In addition, hunters wanted to hunt and to have abundant game. Rather than merely expanding refuges where animals were protected *from* hunting, Leopold reciprocally rejoined with the alternative that more, smaller refuges could protect game *for* hunting by encouraging the overflow of animals into surrounding areas.

In 1928, Leopold took a research position that allowed him to test the hypothesized consequences of his own proposal. He applied scientific forest management principles to wildlife. He studied the past and present conditions of animals and their habitats. Then, he asked what might have caused any changes in population numbers. The collected evidence pointed to several habitat-related factors, besides hunting, that influenced game numbers. It followed that if these other factors could be manipulated by refuge managers to increase populations, then hunters could benefit from the desired overflow of "game animals." Before Leopold's new evidence was published, he wrote and paid a visit to Hornaday, seventy-three years old and bedbound. Leopold wanted his elder to "know first hand" about his new research. He asked his old mentor to "give me a chance" for another visit, before declaring any potential disapprovals in public. Hornaday, holding fast both to his opinion and to his respect for his young colleague, agreed (Warren, 2016: 108).

Five years later, findings contrary to his old friend and mentor's understanding became embedded in Leopold's *Game Management*, a standard university textbook for over a generation. Before the publication of the textbook, Leopold had again courteously communicated with Hornaday. In an April 1933 letter, rebuttals to the side, Leopold thanked him for his past guidance. "My whole venture into this field," Leopold said, "dates from your visit to Albuquerque in 1915 and subsequent encouragement to stay in it" (Warren, 2016: 103, 126).

If Aldo Leopold were still alive, I would ask him, in turn, "to give me a chance." I would want to talk over any disagreements with my evidence-linked valuations opposing his narratives' intergenerational bequest of white supremacist settler-colonial assumptions. I would want to discuss, for instance, why I do not find evidence of him challenging Hornaday's oppressive and racist views, which were very outspoken (1913, Cryer, 2015), nor examining and rejecting versions of his own? I would listen carefully for his response. Whatever that might be; I would also thank him for his past guidance. "Dear Mr. Leopold," I might write, "My whole venture into this field considering 'land health,' expressing my affection for land while 'hewing to the facts' as a scientist and community member, dates from my attention to your writings in 2000."

I have listened to Leopold speaking from the dead long and hard. I also have listened hard to and loved deeply his daughter Nina Leopold Bradley, a mentor and dear friend while she was living and who also has passed on (Warren, 2011). These ancestral voices encourage me to stay in this conversation. Their voices encourage me to keep doing better. Now, "doing better" means not only saying "yes" but saying "no, *and* ..." to crucial aspects, particularly of the canonized Leopoldian legacy.[40] It means responding to Leopoldian proposals with avowals and renewals, but also with firm refusals to repeat ancestral structural-relational, settler-colonial oppressions. "Doing better" furthermore means we settlers first learn how to listen respectfully to Indigenous, Black and others oppressed by this dominating legacy, as itself a reciprocal rejoinder – for instance, attuning, with openness to *not* know, to Indigenous refusals of colonization; to frontlines leadership towards desired futures; and to possible diplomatic Indigenous callings-in to just and responsible relations and more stable and skillful earth-caring coalitions.[41]

2.1.4 Avowing "Intellectual Humility" to Refuse Settler-Colonialism

In the essay Leopold had intended to conclude *A Sand County Almanac*, the writer defined wilderness in multiple senses including as "a resource which can shrink but not grow" (1949: 199) and, in terms of political geography, as an area that is self-maintaining (196), that is, not intentionally directed by human beings. In his closing words, Leopold projected a sweeping role for wilderness (Leopold, 1949: 200):

> Ability to see the cultural value of wilderness boils down, in the last analysis, to a question of intellectual humility. The shallow-minded modern who has lost his rootage in the land assumes that he has already discovered what is important; it is such who prate of empires, political or economic, that will last a thousand years. It is only the scholar who appreciates that all history consists of successive excursions from a single-starting point, to which man returns again and again to organize yet another search for a durable scale of values. It is only the scholar who understands why the raw wilderness gives definition and meaning to the human enterprise.[42]

Although he does not cite T.S. Eliot's poem, Leopold's conclusion resonates with "Little Gidding" (1943), where the poet feels a way through the world war's violent disruptions. As in the aftermath of an explosion, perhaps the poem evokes a sense of the strangeness of once-familiar things, while pointing

---

[40] Perhaps even finding alternatives to the binary of a right or wrong thing.
[41] Warren, J. (2021). "learning dead birdsong, learning first to listen," www.colorado.edu/project/environmental-futures/lecture-archive.
[42] Leopold had intended his essay titled "Wilderness," bearing the quotation, to conclude *A Sand County Almanac*. In the wake of his death, however, colleagues and family members chose "The Land Ethic" to conclude his posthumously published book (Ribbens, 1987: 91–109).

hopefully toward the resumption of more stable times in the midst of uncertainty:

> We shall not cease from exploration
> And the end of all our exploring
> Will be to arrive where we started
> And know the place for the first time.

In both texts, the writer returns to a "single starting point" for a renewal of previous experiences and, at the same time, a fresh start. Leopold's scholar-explorer – a well-meaning, reflective, thinking person – in another arrival might come to see that the place of return is altered beyond recognition, piles of rubble or eroded into the sea, or, that empire or wilderness was only, in the first place, ever a poorly invented conceptual category superimposed on human beings and geography. Correcting for the latter surely would call for avowing "intellectual humility" and, in its renewal, a deep ontological revision of humility itself along with other relational values wrapped up with deceitful fabrications.

Returning to these words that Leopold, before his death, had intended to conclude *A Sand County Almanac*, leads again to paradox, one involving avowals, refusals, and reciprocative rejoinders. Retrieving Leopold's adaptive process of "return," I renew his "question of intellectual humility" in terms of teachability. Openness to un/learning led Leopold to some still-important even "radical" critiques of U.S. dominating culture, including contemporary forms of conservation that were, for instance, "too late ... [and] too little" (Warren, 2016: xxv). Yet white supremacy impairs the virtues of us it privileges and avoids reckoning with how closed off we are to the reality of our offenses. So, at the same time, following Leopold's footsteps requires me, joining with those cited earlier and many others, to refuse his "single starting point" of the so-called "raw wilderness" as an expression of "intellectual humility." Whereas, it is an arrogance of racist colonialist fantasy tied with manifest destiny justified by the doctrine of discovery.

This refusal also, again, returns me to key norms that I failed to surface critically in my own past "land health" scholarship. As I grapple with shifting away from core assumptions of my ancestral-ethical perspective, I turn toward keeping in focus the institution-structuring relationships between chattel slavery, land theft, eugenics, and genocide. On the way to exchanging these unjust ancestral proposals for just and caring alternatives, I mean to reciprocatively rejoinder in listening to attune with lived experiences, knowledges, and desired futures shared by Black and Indigenous and more frontline experts.

Leopold spent his career as a scientist trying to refuse and unlearn destructive land-uses and learn how "to live on a piece of land without spoiling it" (Flader and Callicott, 1991: 249–254). Based on his writings, his adaptive process was part of a continuous cycle of hypothesis-making and hypothesis testing – a pattern of imaginative guessing and ground-truthing reality checks. Throughout his career, Leopold showed not only that he could sometimes change others' minds but also his own, as might be warranted by new, convincing evidence (Leopold, 1949: 129–133; Warren, 2016: 126). As his close colleague, the English ecologist and author F. Fraser Darling, observed, Leopold "was always seeing and learning" (Warren, 2016: xxix). Indeed, Leopold's intellectual humility, more so than "raw wilderness," is renewable at least to a degree. His teachability might also itself remain a reciprocative rejoinder to his elders' and ancestors' imperial culture – challenging how particular core cultural values were expressed and/or those very values themselves.

One example of how Leopold's fresh insights challenged how a core value was expressed, but not the value itself emerges from that early disagreement with Hornaday. Leopold and Hornaday never disagreed over care for "wild things" and the need to protect threatened forms of life. Leopold was, rather, interested in updating his mentor's approach to doing so. In another instance, Leopold's ongoing self-education led him to quit participating in a widespread federal project to exterminate wolves to reduce livestock and game losses. Leopold had both awakened to an individual wolf's beauty and learned more about ecological relationships of the canids within their communities, a double insight recorded in "Thinking Like a Mountain" (Leopold, 1949: 129–133). He also found evidence that without wolves, deer populations spiked and browsed their forests faster than plants and soils could regenerate, leaving all, including human hunters, without sustenance. This new information did not establish his affection for land, which was pre-existing. It informed his skill in expressing it.

At other times, however, results of Leopold's explorations of land led him to challenge some common assumptions of his heritage or core values themselves. For instance, he observed the consequences of livestock overgrazing eroding the life-sustaining capacities of the U.S. Southwest. A decade later, he witnessed the midwestern "Dust Bowl," caused proximately by wheat overcropping (Warren, 2016: 252–253). As he dug deeper into ultimate causes, his experiences led him to refuse some major land-relationship norms – ones involving environmental fracturings of humans and nature – of the U.S. settler-colonial economy. One of these fracturing norms was the prioritization of a commodity value of land to accommodate capitalists' insistence on increasing wealth (Warren, 2016: 248). The standard of capitalism, Leopold came to understand, undermined not only "the cultural values of wilderness" and long-term land-community health, as he saw it, but also, eventually, the future profits and prospects of even the most comfortable profiteers.

Leopold often followed critiques of his culture with impressive alternatives. He so-rejoindered his refusals of inherited cultural habits, as I detailed in *Odyssey*, by series of frameworks and methodologies – innovative within U.S. conservation history – from scientific forestry to game management, including the protective political designations of refuges and wilderness areas. Moreover, Leopold developed his land ethic hand in hand with his intra-culturally challenging vision of land health. Leopold took wilderness, in the latter case, to be the "most perfect norm" (Leopold, 1949: 196) for land doctoring (Callicott and Freyfogle, 1999: 220). As we saw at the opening of this section, wilderness was the "starting point" to which "man returns again and again to organize yet another search for a durable scale of values."

Yet in none of Leopold's returns to "raw wilderness" as a values source is there evidence that his teachability extended to humble refusal nor unlearning of this concept itself as an unverifiable abstraction. For all his deep thinking, Leopold did not reciprocate with a rejoinder that would transform or supersede the specious idea, raising serious questions about the validity of scientific research – to date – that takes it as a reference point. Leopold's narratives do not disavow "wilderness" as involving rote repetition of his settler-colonialist ancestors' violent disrespect for and relegations of "other" human beings from their homelands. They do not refuse the arrogant cruelty to Indigenous Peoples nor the ways in which the U.S. capitalist economy has always been tied to African slaves working stolen lands nor to the injustices wrought by warring empires cold movements of persons and/or political borders. To recognize this – happening right before his and other white settlers' eyes – might have moved intellects of "progress" to prevent "broken" land and tend to human-land "harmony" (1949: 153) as tied with the also systemic alienation of some human beings from full dignity and their eliminations from their ecologies. It would have meant facing the need for the radical healing of the colonial fracture operating in Euro-American land-use assumptions, structures, and practices. It would have led to contesting, moreover, the founding U.S. national narratives weaving into dominating, settler scientific institutions and research conclusions, weaving into the conservation movement including still-influential Leopoldian notions, and weaving into later environmental and sustainability movements and the institutions and policies arising from them, with ongoing consequences.

2.2 Avowing Solidarity to Refuse Hegemony: A Method of Anti/Colonialist-Indigenous Narrative Comparisons

As part of his intellectual and ethical development, Leopold grew aware of power-diminishing fragmentation within the U.S. conservation movement in his lifetime. For example, he wrote about inner-conservation conflicts between sustained-yield foresters, ecological researchers, recreationists, and hunters (e.g., Warren, 2016: 104–105, 349). In addition to helping lead Leopold to perceive land elements as interconnected, the need to respect the differences in land-use emphases led him to try coalition-building. He thus did not urge merging "*organizations* so much as *rationales* for preserving wilderness" (Warren, 2008: 99). Perhaps a society at constant odds with itself might come together in the search for a wilderness-informed, shared "durable scale of values." Returning to this arena now, yet again, there may be much in Leopold's legacy to avow. At the same time, the ideas of shared values and coalitions of interests raise questions of how best to orient within "differences that make a difference" (Ruíz and Dotson, 2017: 2, 13). Moreover, any good renewals of ancestral proposals of solidarity must first reckon with their context of settler-colonial white supremacy including manifest destiny.

If there is any chance of creating coalitions durable enough to support meaningful, just climate and land protection, Leopoldian conservationists cannot mistake Heglar's and Demientieff's generous care for others as an excuse to forget that these land issues are Black and Indigenous issues. Again, it calls for Black feminisms philosopher Kristie Dotson's keeping *in focus* "politics of elimination" of "settler-slave-native relations" (Dotson, 2018: 195). To make good relations, in other words, as Quechua descendant and collaborative researcher Andrea Vásquez-Fernández and Ahtahkakoop Cree Nation member and Canada Research Chair Cash Ahenakew pii tai poo taa (flying eagle) write, potential non-Indigenous allies and accomplices with Indigenous Peoples will acknowledge the "incommensurability of clashing 'notions'" (2020: 65–70). We will cease privileging "Western" paradigms like "sustainable development" that reproduce settler-colonial exploitation of "Mother Earth," of Native lands, and that lead to the genocides of Indigenous Peoples and more of non-dominating identities. Those calls seem applicable to traditional land-relational English-language terms such as "conservation" itself, "environmentalism," and "wilderness protection," and, as an ongoing reminder, regarding uses of "climate justice" and even "just transition." These authors also stress attending to "the limitations of what we cannot imagine from our entrenched westernized frames of reference and/or intercultural equivocality" (65). More exists in "desired futures" than anyone – particularly "we" settlers – can dream up from a position within a dominating culture[43]

---

[43] See also Burkhart, 2019; Tallbear, 2019 (quoting Nick Estes term "settler ontocide"); Whyte, 2017a; Whyte, 2018b.

Directly regarding Leopold's ongoing conservation legacy, Kyle Powys Whyte specifies the need, in any attempts to bring different heritages together, to daylight underlying differences in any comparisons of Leopoldian ethical orientations and Indigenist ones (2015, 2024). He explains that while there is the chance of convergence of insights from distinct origins, such cannot be determined without paying close attention to differences among "notions" and the challenges of translation. Here, too, such crucial differences, especially if left buried, will fester into ongoing suppression, violence, and bad history (Whyte, personal communication, 2021). These hidden differences would undermine chances for any genuine and sustainable Indigenous-settler-conservationist coalitions.

With this in mind, I return to Whyte's three pithy issues of deep Leopoldian-Indigenist comparisons that "must be reckoned with" (2015: 2, 2024). This would be on the way to bringing P/people(s) together around any genuinely complementary if not commensurate land-ethical orientations. One troubling difference is that Leopold's morally ascendant narrative of "all history" (1949: 200) is partial, biased, and unsound. It is "the exact reverse" ethical unfolding experienced by many Native Peoples by force of colonization (Whyte, 2015: 13, 2024). This includes acknowledging a brutal irony. Leopold's tale indifferently imposes settler-colonial guilt and possible self-redemption on many Indigenous Peoples. While settler-colonialists ourselves – including via Leopold's land health vision – *are* guilty of systemically obstructing Indigenous ecologies and collective continuance and often with "negative environmental consequences" (Whyte, 2015: 13) for everyone. For instance, continual threats to some 370 million Indigenous persons who "live on 22 percent of the world's land surface" also threaten "about 80 percent of the planet's biodiversity" (Sobrevila, 2008: xii). Life is tied to these lands and with Indigenous ethics and "knowledge systems" already composed with "anti-colonial action" and "critical feedback loops" (Whyte, 2024).

Another problem, following Whyte, are the differences between how Leopold (and those decision-makers, institutions, and policies shaped by Leopold's concepts) and various Indigenous Tribes and First Nations enact(ed) their land-relational norms. This matter involves delving into settler presumptions of theoretical ethical similarities, in the abstract, that turn out to be dissimilar or even incommensurable ethics in practice (Tuck and Yang, 2012; Whyte, 2015, 2024). For example, as Whyte discusses, whereas Leopold's words and some of his projects challenge commodification, his home and work ventures do not model re-structured power relations nor economic and justice-determined changes. On the other hand, Anishinaabe women elders' Mother Earth Water Walk enacts responsibilities to water that are "part and parcel of maintaining family/kin, community and ceremonial relationships across species" (Whyte, 2024). And, in courageously demonstrating their culture's self-organization of reciprocal responsibilities, the Walk effectively re-sets unjust configurations of the dominating settler state (Whyte 2015, 2024).

A third comparison is between an epistemological framework that vests authority in Leopold's land ethic and other channels that represent equitable dependence upon Indigenous knowledge systems (e.g., for decision-making), on their Peoples' own terms. In Whyte's analysis, privileging Leopoldian land-ethical norms, such as land health rooted in a wilderness concept, as the host or "translator of Indigenous ethics" can "grant unsubstantiated and even offensive privilege" (2015: 2–3, 2024). As we will see, prioritizing the land ethic legacy sanctions ongoing colonial "cruelty," which settlers ourselves know (Merchant, 1989; Cronon, 1996: 15), toward Indigenous Peoples, undermining their sovereignties, also so-inflicting Black and Brown and more who are marginalized.

All three of Whyte's comparisons ask, more generally, *who* gets to decide? Who, with what values, is procedurally suppressed (in advance) in decision-making processes, and who benefits from the suppression? Further, what can we learn from potentially reciprocal (e.g., epistemic, intergenerational, ancestral, kinship) land ethical dependencies? Broadly, these comparisons keep *in focus*, for the sake of refusing and reciprocally rejoindering, the U.S. settler agenda of (1) *human relegations* – forcible removals and/or dispossessions of Indigenous Peoples, Black persons, Latinas/os, and more racialized as non-white (that is, as in the way) from/ lands, including by murder, abduction, relocation, and moving political boundaries; (2) *"resource" appropriations"* – thefts of land and waters and elements extracted from them, also pilfering alluring elements of colonized cultures to benefit empire; and 3) *forced assimilations* of P/people/s to "the" norms of (already privileged) "white" (Euro-American, abled, male/heteropatriarchal) society.

3 Refusing Leopoldian Settler-Colonial Proposals

These three interactively emergent foci – relegations, appropriations, assimilations – appear within my method of critical narrative praxis, which is organized by Whyte's "three serious issues that must be reckoned with" in any attempts to stabilize Indigenous-settler/Leopoldian environmental coalitions, involving: (1) reverse histories, (2) different land ethical norms, and (3) non-reciprocal epistemic dependence. This method meshes with my Harrison-informed, intergenerational, and conversational methodology. Following from my above partial renewals of Leopold's own forms of intergenerational respect, teachability with intellectual humility, and solidarity, I continue to retrieve

Leopoldian proposals to refuse their white supremacist settler-colonial and oppressive offenses. In a following section, again corresponding to Whyte's three issues, I reciprocate the refused proposals with a rejoinder of respectfully and actively listening (for understanding, including *not* knowing) to proposals of Gwich'in and other Alaska Native land citizens and protectors. I apply this potentially ontologically transformative matrix of methodology, method, and foci in support of more stable coalitions of groups with common concerns while noticing-to-respect important differences on the way to desired futures. This Element's ongoing narrative "excursion" includes troubling and re-troubling "wilderness" (conceptually and politically) as "a single starting point to which man returns again and again" and the durability of the "scale of values" rising from it, and, thus, of anything incorporating it without such attention, including Leopold's normative land health concept. It becomes clear that this narrative circling leads, repeatedly, to a nowhere that gives rise to values reflecting Indigenous disappearances. This Element concludes in support of settler listening as responsibly attuning, in actively unsettling ways, to Indigenous-led proposals, particularly working toward decolonization and liberation for all. It encourages us settlers to "stay in it."

3.1 Bad History: The Flip Side of Virtue

One overall and repeating narrative arc of Leopold's *A Sand County Almanac*, from the Foreword to the penultimate essay, "Wilderness," and what became the final essay, "The Land Ethic," proposes moral ascension. Settlers rise from land-conquering "pioneers" to conservationists, becoming "land doctors" for "land health," and promoting mental and spiritual health by expanding land community-mindedness. Leopold imagines a scheme, in Whyte's incisive words, that "will redeem Euro-American people from the historical destruction of the environment that they have caused" (Whyte, 2024). And Leopold nonchalantly imposes his colonizing narrative even on abducted and enslaved Black persons, Native Land citizens, Latinas/os living "goodlife" relations (Ybarra, 2016), folded into that historical destruction, by violent tactics of relegation, appropriation, and assimilation.

In the Foreword to his best-selling book, Leopold introduces himself as part of (an already warm and well-fed) minority – those who prefer "wild things" over "progress" (Leopold, 1949: vii–ix). Mainstream progress is defined as an increasing pile of money and the "material blessings" it buys, including televisions and multiple bathtubs, as well as land as "property." "Wild things" encompass winds, sunsets, geese, and pasque flowers. In "Wilderness" (188–201), Leopold reinforces his arguments on behalf of these "things" beyond human re/creation – as he had since the start of his career under the influence of Hornaday. In "Wilderness," Leopold urges reasons for protecting "the raw material out of which man has hammered the artifact called civilization" (188). In his narrative, the wilderness-conquering pioneer turns anvil-pounding laborer coming into a moment of "repose." In this repose, the builders of civilization should appreciate the "raw material" they are made of while there is still any remaining, Leopold writes. Civilized persons need not view "wilderness" as an "adversary," Leopold proposes. Pioneers turned laborers able to have some leisure and desiring adventure, as well as material provisions, would do well to appreciate all remaining sizes and degrees of "wildness" (189) as "something to be loved and cherished, because it gives definition and meaning to [their] life" (188).

As we have seen, cherishing more-than-human-lives was something Leopold and Hornaday maintained agreement on even while disagreeing on how best to protect wildlife and wildlife habitat, including the larger most "wild" wilderness regions supporting big carnivores like grizzly bears (Hornaday 1913: 156; Leopold 1949: 198). Likewise, Leopold continued resonating with Hornday's "racial animus" (Cryer, 2015: 500) in ways that would forcefully and unjustly assimilate Indigenous people into settler "pioneer" narratives of land protective or ethical behavior which was to relegate them from their own lands, disrupting traditions of kinship responsibilities. For instance, Hornaday in his 1913 *Vanishing Wildlife* wrote that "The Indian should have no game advantages whatever over a white man" (176). He called for "Indians," many with treaties promising hunting rights, to "obey the general game laws, just the same as white men" (176, also Cryer, 2015: 499). And Leopold's early-career game protective work in the U.S. Southwest had promoted hunting restrictions that denied "customary hunting freedoms" of "Indians" (i.e., Diné/Navajo, Apache, Puebloan Peoples), whom some settlers also blamed, along with predatory wolves, for game declines (Warren, 1993: 83; see also Leopold 1949: 191). As American environmental historian Louis S. Warren discusses, there was more than wildlife protection under the surface of emerging game laws. Supporters, including Leopold, proposed to enact free and democratic equity in hunting access. Yet, according to Warren, the laws also brought competing "Anglos and Hispanos" – many of the latter themselves dispossessed by U.S. treaty-breaking – into coalition "to push Indians off their lands" and appropriate them, including into conservation's hands (1993: 83, 92, 94, 97).

In a conceptually similar way, decades later and not having disavowed his mentor's racism, Leopold, the university professor and conservation statesman, continued assimilating Indigenous people into his story of the would-be ethical progress of the pioneer, incorporating settler notions of outdoor recreation (1949: 179). To support his claim that "wild game is no longer necessary as 'food,'"

Hornaday had written in 1913 that "In the United States, the day of the hungry Indian-fighting pioneer had gone by and there is an abundance of food everywhere" (310). "Physical combat for the means of subsistence ... as an economic fact," Leopold wrote in "Wilderness," had "disappeared as such" (192). As he had noted in the *Almanac's* Foreword, outdoor survival had been replaced by "the assurance [by mechanization] of a good breakfast" (vii).

Hunting and fishing remained critical to Leopold in another way, however, as "a means of perpetuating, in sport form, the more virile and primitive skills in pioneering travel and subsistence" (192). The importance of certain types of outdoor recreation, which you might "know in your bones" (or as "atavistic instincts," see Warren 2016: 282), went to the "wild roots" of culture, in Leopold's terms (177). And the "cultural values" of wilderness recreation included stimulating "awareness of history" or "'nationalism' in its best sense" (177); "elemental man-earth relation," and "voluntary limitation" on use of tools called "sportsmanship" (178). Toward these gains, Leopold praised not only hunting and fishing, but especially canoe travel and travel by pack-train as key "primitive skills" American-style. At the same time, slantwise, he encouraged restrictions on the experience-foiling and wide-spreading "tune of motor launches." And Leopold blamed, in particular, "Your Hudson Bay Indian"[44] who "now has a put-put" (193) and whose reasons for using it were their own. With his offhand, condescending complaint, Leopold assimilated Indigenous Peoples into his narrative of the ongoing, inevitable, modern, and industrialized "world-wide hybridization of cultures" (188) into which his idea of conservation must intervene. And Leopold so-relegated the awareness of structural injustice along with the awareness of histories, nationalisms, traditional food relationships, and ways of life of multiple Indigenous Nations and Tribes, while regulating their self-determination and appropriating control of Indigenous lands and of the values of so-called "primitive skills" (Deloria, 2022: 101).

In addition to the wilderness values of recreation (prioritizing performative facets of pioneering life "to be more like the very people they were excluding," Cryer: 2015: 498) and for establishing refuges for especially large and threatened species (e.g., "Alaskan [grizzly] bears"), Leopold discussed two other key

---

[44] Likely referring to any members of multiple Indigenous Nations and Tribes (including Cree, Inuit, and Gwich'in) involved in/by the huge, complex fur-trading network of the Hudson's Bay Company established in the seventeenth century. The HBC appropriated some 5 million square miles of geography in what became Canada and the northwestern U.S. The HBC took economic control of some Indigenous communities, including Ojibwe ones, persisting into the late twentieth century (Gismondi, M. (2022). "The Untold Story of the Hudson's Bay Company," https://canadiangeographic.ca/articles/the-untold-story-of-the-hudsons-bay-company/.; Honeyman, D. (2003). "Indian Trappers and the Hudson's Bay Company," https://journals.librarypublishing.arizona.edu/arizanthro/article/id/464/.

justifications to preserve "wilderness" in his essay "Wilderness" of the *Almanac*. There was the value of "tag-ends" or "museum pieces" of land, which may include small and even human-occupied remnants (for generations to experience "the origins of their cultural inheritance," 188–92). And, as previously noted, there was the value of preserving wilderness for science (as a "base datum of normality ... of how healthy land maintains itself as an organism," 194–98). These categories of wilderness value crescendo into Leopold's proposal to take wilderness, all in all, as that "single starting point," a source where the search for "a durable scale of values" re-sets repeatedly.[45]

Besides assimilation of Indigenous people into the recreational value of wilderness, there was overlap between the value of preserving "tag-ends" of wilderness and of North American tribes, in Leopold's thinking. For example, among remnants worth preserving were "the last little fragment" of Pueblo "Indian culture" (Flader and Callicott, 1991: 102)[46] and "the last Seminole culture, the last wild eastern cougar, and one of the last groups of pure eastern turkey."[47] In the cases both of Pueblo Peoples and Seminole, defense of their "last" was against threats of destruction of land and "wild things" by profit-driven industrialization against which his ideas of conservation stood. Leopold justified protecting the Pueblo fragment because "the Creator" made "mankind, in his image" (Flader and Callicott, 1991: 102). This was similar to his arguments to respect all that was God-made (96) or evolved by "Nature" (Warren, 2016: 94) and for the safe-keeping all the "parts" of land[48] and of *"the greatest possible variety"* of "indigenous" animals (1933: 403). Leopold's tag-end arguments did not, however, acknowledge the collective continuance of the nineteen Pueblo Nations – from Acoma to Zuni – including fierce opposition to Spanish and U.S. colonization. "The Pueblo Indians ... civilization expired, but not because their land expired," Leopold commented blankly in his *Almanac* (207).

---

[45] Powell (2015), says: "By reiterating the myth of wilderness-as-Nordic-frontier Leopold helped perpetuate an enduring divide between America's environmental movement and the nation's nonwhite citizenry" (202).

[46] Leopold wrote, in 1923, against the further "disintegration of the Pueblo Indian communes" by the 1921 Bursum Bill. This would have allowed settlers to claim more Pueblo land. Leopold's particular complaint, though, was against "the ultimate impertinence" of "boosterism," that is, the drive for profit-making, including from tourists visiting a Pueblo's "distinctive culture" (Flader and Callicott, 102; see Soliz, S. (2019). "Pueblo Activists," https://sarweb.org/pueblo-activists-and-allies-against-the-bursum-bill-of-1921/. A year after Leopold's writing, in 1924 (after the Allotment Act had privatized and reduced Indigenous land access), U.S. citizenship was extended to all Indigenous persons.

[47] Leopold (1941). Letter to Senate Committee on Indian Affairs, LP 9/25/10-2, 4(2): 72-3.

[48] Leopold. (November 23, 1938). "Lecture: "Economics, Philosophy, and Land," LP 9/25/10-6, 16(5): 534–8).

Leopold's justification for including Seminole in his list of "wild resources" also was strategic. Protecting them overlapped with protecting deer upon which the "last easterly remnant of cougar depended" (Leopold, 1940). Romantic and condescending arguments might even have some positive consequences, for instance, supporting some Pueblo peoples' survival, giving Seminole ecology some protection, maintaining, and/or expanding (under the 1934 Indian Reorganization Act) some Reservation lands, at least in the short run (Taffa, 2024: 70).[49] They did not deeply align with Indigenous Seminole self-determination, however. Seminole, already with every reason to maintain suspicion of and resistance to colonialist treachery (Philip, 1977), had told officials that the deer of their Reservation did not have ticks (Komarek, 1941).[50] Nonetheless the Seminole were beset by feuding U.S. agency men and conservation scientists (including supported by Leopold). The officials appeared with their own agendas, insistent on proving or disproving the presence of ticks themselves, destabilizing U.S. government efforts to rebuild trust.

A key value of wilderness for Leopold was for science: to keep a "laboratory" of healthy land "organisms" to study in order to diagnose lands "deranged" and "sickened" by pioneering and its aftermath and to guide efforts in healing them. For this purpose, Leopold proposes "two available norms." The first is land occupied by humans, for centuries, yet wherein the "land physiology remains largely normal." Leopold claims to know of "only one such place," naming "north-eastern Europe" (Leopold, 1949: 149–153).[51] Yet, on the following

---

[49] Leopold. (March 6, 1940). Letter to Secretary Harold Ickes, LP 9/25/10-2, 4(2): 221. Bureau of Indian Affairs Commissioner, John Collier, supported "Indians" as possessing "long-lost, unrecoverable wilderness heritage" connected with their "spiritual life" (Philip, 1977: 28). Historian Paul Sutter (2002: 3–4) argues that New Deal work projects precipitated the co-founding of the Wilderness Society, including by Leopold. As evidence that Collier shared concern for wilderness protection, he was also invited into this small founding group. Perhaps because Collier had been recently appointed to head the BIA, he declined it. The Leopold Papers' "Florida Deer Tick Controversy" folders provide more detailed context than can be summarized here. As one more example of condescension to Seminole, however, see E.V. Komarek to Collier, Sept 4, 1941 in which Komarek urges "actually developing game as a resource for Indians." He thought that "game could be developed and managed just as surely as agricultural crops and other things we try to make the Indians do." As to being strategic (as a member of an inner circle), Leopold, in a Sept 18, 1941 letter, praises Komarek's rhetoric to Collier. "I am particularly pleased to have you steer up the question of Indian game as a declining resource," Leopold writes. "I think Collier will get your point" (LP 9/25/10-2, 4[2]: 54–6).

[50] Komarek, R. (Oct. 1, 1941). "Confidential Report on South Florida Deer-Fever Tick Investigation," LP 9/25/10-2, 4(2): 46–53. For pluses and minuses and influences on and of Collier's New Deal era Indian Reform Act see Wolfe, 2006; Genetin-Pilawa, C.J., 2012; Taffa, 2024, and many more.

[51] Leopold's naming "north-eastern Europe" here is odd in two ways. First, it is north-western Europe he points to in "The Land Ethic," which is also where he had made his own observations. (See also "Biotic Land-use," Callicott and Freyfogle, 1999: 203.) Second, perhaps Leopold felt the lands along the Rio Gavilan across the U.S. border in Mexico were also doomed to industrial settlement. Yet, in other writings, he waxed eloquent about how these lands presented "so lovely

page, without so-exalting it, he describes another example – the trout-filled and mossy-banked "Sierra Madre of Chihuahua, never grazed or used [by Euro-American settlers] for fear of [warring] Indians." That is, although obviously well occupied by humans – Apache Tribes – readers are left to infer that Leopold relegates Apache outside his meaning of "human" in order to appropriate the flourishing area into what he calls the "Sierra Madre *wilderness*" (italics mine). Leopold then praises this "wilderness" as "a norm for the cure of sick land on both sides of the [Mexican-U.S.] border," and, moreover, a "good-neighbor enterprise" (Leopold, 1949: 197).

The second "most perfect [land health] norm," Leopold says, "is wilderness," or, "virgin country" (Leopold, 1949: 191, 196). As examples, Leopold defines swaths of so-called Canada and Alaska by quoting (imperfectly and, again, without citation) "To the Man of the High North" by poet Robert Service: "Where nameless men by nameless rivers wander/And in strange valleys die strange deaths alone."[52] "To those devoid of imagination," Leopold wrote in "Conservation Esthetic," "a blank place on the map is a useless waste; to others, the most valuable part," holding up Alaska as a prime example (1949: 176). Service's gold "moilers" aside, "a blank place," whether viewed as useless or valuable, relegates from settler imaginations how "Alaska" is a geography, formerly occupied by Russia and then by the U.S., but unceded by self-determining Indigenous Nations and Tribes. It suppresses how Alaska Natives have originated at least twenty local languages with which to map their own homelands. It covers over those who have skillfully adapted and thrived across this vast area for time immemorial, "over the millennia" (e.g., Mishler and Frank, 2019: 36), who are woven into their own ecologies with attached rights and responsibilities.

"*Nimiqtuumaruq aktunaamik*: bound with a rope. / This land with its laws that serve as wire / and root to draw us together," says Iñupiaq and poet Joan Naviyuk Kane in "Exceeding Beringia" (Smith, 2021: 167–168).[53] Her poem destabilizes any claims to a "land bridge" history of one-way migration of human beings, from Asia to North America. In this mistaken, universalizing narrative, people moved through the Arctic finding "temperate-normative" ideals to the south, as dAXunhyuu (Eyak, Alaska Native) geographer Jen Rose Smith discusses (2021: 159–160).[54] That history, too, told by "Natural

---

a picture of ecological health" and "virgin stability." He used the term "virgin," though he knew these were human-occupied Lands. See also Flader & Callicott, 1991: 239–244.

[52] Service, R. (1909). *Ballads of a Cheechako*, /www.gutenberg.org/files/259/259-h/259-h.htm.

[53] Kane, J. (2016). "Exceeding Beringia," https://poets.org/poem/exceeding-beringia.

[54] And Smith, J.R. (2022). "Racialization and Resistance in the Ice Geographies of the Arctic and Colonized Alaska, https://thefunambulist.net/magazine/the-land/racialization-and-resistance-in-the-ice-geographies-of-the-arctic-and-colonized-alaska.

Historians," repeats imaginaries relegating Peoples of the Arctic and other cold places – dAXunhyuu, Iñupiat, Gwich'in and the many more. Despite colonialist efforts otherwise, they retain their own creation stories – "emergences, transits, and arrivals" – and are actors in "the History of the World" with the highest attainments of "the human mind," Smith writes (162, 163, 165), in terms counter to racialized, environmentally deterministic claims. And, despite cultural fissures wreaked also by assimilative acts, such as by-force English-only boarding schools, Alaska Native Peoples have many names for themselves and for rivers and other features of their albeit appropriated geographies (Raboff, 2001; Baldwin, et al., 2018).[55]

There is, for instance, "the *Kuzitrun*," as Kane writes (in Smith, 167–168),

> drained by inland veins scrawling tributaries
> with name upon vanishing name.
> The giant granite tors at Serpentine:
> Iyat, the cooking pot sentineled
> by unscoured stone as it towers

"Let us lose our grief," Kane continues a few lines later, "in great rafts as we translate the renamed // straits."

"Ability to see the cultural value of wilderness boils down, in the last analysis, to a question of intellectual humility," Leopold wrote (1949: 200). As I reconsider his senses of value, I can renew my cultural ancestor's affection for more-than-humankinds. I still avow his human hearts-motivating resistance to commodifying-industrial extractive land wreckage. At the same time, revisioning Leopoldian value, I disavow his presumptuous, grand narrative – of historical moral ascendancy normalized in "wilderness" hand-in-hand with "land health." Counter to his proposal of humility, these concepts demonstrate no change in thinking about ancestral racism and entitled authority. His grand historical narrative builds from Euro-(colonizing) pioneer to (settler) laborer-in-repose, to land-wanderer and healer who gains "definition and meaning." At the same time, paradoxically, his settler-colonialist story effects relegation of many Native Peoples from full human stature and off their homelands also removing their place names from maps, appropriates their customary territories, and assimilates Native Peoples disrupting ecologies, cultures, languages, and values, as we shall see in yet further examples. Leopold's tale also vanishes, by condescending or no mention, generations of enslaved Black

---

[55] Alaska Native Language Center, "Languages," www.uaf.edu/anlc/; For example, Gwich'in Social and Cultural Institute, *Gwich'in Place Names Atlas*, https://atlas.gwichin.ca/index.html.

lives, dispossessed Latinas/os, Chinese, and more "non-white" identities (Savoy, 2015: 33).[56]

In "The Land Ethic" of his *Almanac*, Leopold offers a succinct yet detailed narrative of settler-colonial deliverance into the world of the land ethic. He expounds "The Ethical Sequence" with origins in "Odysseus' Greece," the hero's killing of his wife Penelope's suitors, and the murder of disloyal "slave girls." From that violently punishing beginning, Leopold sketches a history "of three thousand years" of an extending "ethical structure." Improving on the ancients, not only men but, he implies, women and "human chattels" have become morally encompassed. From relations between individuals, ethics have expanded to include those between individuals and society and vice versa in this tale. The next needed ethical step, Leopold proposes, looking to the future, is from "man" to "soils, waters, plants, and animals, or collectively: the land," for which he takes "wilderness" as the most perfect norm of settler-occupied land health.

As seen throughout this section, this land health vision relegates Indigenous Peoples out of "wildernesses," appropriates the lands they belong to, and assimilates Indigenous and other diverse cultures into a tale of "world-wide hybridization," unprecedented "in the history of the human species" (Leopold, 1949: 118, 218). Leopold's historical ethical narrative of a much-needed moral ascension also folds everyone into it, as Whyte underscores, many without consent. "*All* ethics so far evolved," Leopold writes, "rest upon a *single* premise: that the individual is a member of a community of interdependent parts" [italics mine (203)]. A healthy "land community," to Leopold's assimilative perception, "changes the role of *Homo sapiens* from conqueror to plain member and citizen of it" (204). "There is *as yet no ethic* [italics mine] dealing with man's relation to land and to the animals and plants which grow upon it. Land, like Odysseus's slave girls, is still property. The land relation is still [from the ancient times of Homer's Odysseus] strictly economic, entailing privileges but not obligations" (203). "The extension of ethics" to "the land-relation," Leopold proposes, is "an evolutionary possibility and an ecological necessity" (203). I have needed to stop and reflect further on what that points to.

At my earliest reading of *A Sand County Almanac*, Leopold's narrative trajectory sat uncomfortably with me. Schooled in Calvinism's doctrine of

---

[56] As Lauret Savoy notes in her 2015 book *Trace*, Leopold, understood the power of various forms of suppression. Yet while he attended to "the erasure of Silphium," a flower, he only mentioned in passing the "erasure of a human subspecies," in his words, referring to Chinese people (33; Leopold, 1949: 48). As Savoy underscores, Leopold mentioned "slavery ... human beings as property," but only in reference to the "slave girls" of ancient Greece at Odysseus's banquet (33; Leopold, 1949: 201, 203). Leopold also referred to land as enslaved, yet not Africans and Indigenous and more persons enslaved in/by the U.S. (1949: 223).

original sin, I still questioned faith, generally and personally, in a story of collective human improvement. As a trained scientist, moreover, I understood that evolution by natural selection, after all, isn't about "improvement" of organisms per se but about adaptive changes, across generations, within a population interacting within dynamic local geographies. From the start, I felt how Leopold, far from exhibiting "intellectual humility" or teachability, was overreaching when he wrote in such sweeping terms. Though still ignorant of details I needed to know, and living under a master narrative I had hardly yet recognized, I already knew something was wrong. Feeling your gut and cultivating that kind of knowing is crucial to countering improper and dangerous claims. I wish I had done so far sooner.

As Whyte concludes in his reading of the narrative of moral ascension, "Leopold's history of ethics is based on a narrative the plot of which goes in the opposite direction of the narratives many Indigenous peoples would provide of their ethics." "Many Indigenous people would see the colonialisms of the last 500 years," Whyte says, "as introducing ethics that were less inclusive of non-human entities and collectives." Indigenous Peoples with relations disrupted and land-care responsibilities obstructed by imposed settler-colonialist stories, experiencing violent consequences, Whyte explains, "cannot see themselves in Leopold's historic sequence because they do not see the progression of their societies as moving toward a land ethic; rather, the fear is that their societies are moving away from being societies in which their ethic is fully entrenched in their lifestyles and in the self-governance of their societies and nations" (Whyte, 2024).

3.2 Consequential Ethical Abstractions: Who "Inherits the Earth"?

Leopold's grand historical narrative of self-redemptive cultural and moral ascension not only unfolded in a direction opposite to many Indigenous ethical trajectories experienced under settler-colonialism. It stifled the latter, and its insights, in its sweeping claim to be telling "all history." Similarly, the idea of a common humanity – that is, the biologically based "we" of the "human race" or *Homo sapiens* (Fuentes, et al., 2019) differentiated from other life forms – might be rhetorically appealing in many ways and sometimes appropriate. But, as I earlier acknowledged my own rote repetition of this ancestral proposal, this unspecified "we" can also be a cover for a controlling group to systematically assimilate other groups into itself, an immoral violence that also manifests an imprudent relegation of diversity (Colebrook, 2018). On the other hand, Leopold's ascensional, moral-historical narrative interlocks with relatively recent, false beliefs about human variation masquerading as scientific classification. "Race" is an abstraction with very real consequences used to classify and regulate people as different groups of "others" while upholding white supremacy. As discussed earlier, white supremacy is rooted in pre-existent, resilient, expansionary European settler-colonialism and woven into the fibers of U.S. nationhood structured to appropriate and profit from land (Memmi, 1965; Wolfe, 2006; Tallbear, 2013; Fuentes, et al., 2019; McLean, 2020).

Race "arose as a justification for Euro-Western colonialism and enslavement," according to Queer Trans and Black scientist Shay-Akil McLean (2020: 41). "Race is a product of racism, always," writes McLean (2020: 43) and has "never been wholly innocent, unbiased, or apolitical" (Fuentes et al., 2019: 401). Race is historical in the sense that "race/ism," as a socially constructed and learned system of thought and practices, has *not* existed in all times and places (McLean, 2020: 42). Lauret Savoy observes how Virginia colonists in the Chesapeake region developed their rules of slavery and of race. By the late 1600s they were "referring to themselves as 'white' rather than primarily English or Christian," Savoy says. In this way, European settlers elevated their power over those whose land they would forcibly take – "Patawomeck, Mattaponi, Rappahannock, Powhatan, so many more" lumped into the category "Indian" – and those they had forcibly taken from vast Africa – "Igbo. Ibibio. Moko. Kongo. Wolof. Bamana. Akan. Ga. Others" lumped into "Negro" or "Black." These categories came to mark not only difference but deficiency linked to physical markers such as skin color, Savoy explains.[57]

The erroneous "rigid 'biological' taxonomies of later centuries," as Savoy tells us, "lurched" from this legacy of hierarchical racial categories. Then, in the nineteenth century, ideas about "race" normalized into "a scientific object of inquiry," according to Tallbear (2013: 33). This helped swing the focus away from race as a problem of "difference in power and resources" into baseless assumptions of race as a "problem of difference in phenotype and attitude" (McLean, 2020: 43–44). "Biology," McLean says, "did not recruit race; instead, race and racism recruited biology" into its political aspirations (44). Since there is a before "race," as McLean says, there might also be an afterward. That is, this knowledge points to a future unlearning, an abolishment of race/ism – dismantling the profit-driven, resource-minded, and carceral system and revisioning relationships conjoined with decolonization, including Land Back.[58]

From early in his career to his final writings, Leopold's occupation with defining and expressing good land use brought him repeatedly to his "search for a durable scale of values" informed by "wilderness" (1949: 200). It also raised

---

[57] Savoy, L. (2023). "Ancestral Structures on the Trailing Edge," https://emergencemagazine.org/essay/ancestral-structures-on-the-trailing-edge/.

[58] Morris, C. (2023)., "To Build an Abolitionist Future, We Must Look to Indigenous Pasts," https://truthout.org/articles/to-build-an-abolitionist-future-we-must-look-to-indigenous-pasts/.

multiple manifestations of a troubling question – how to get more people to share in that search? This question, in various formulations, helped motivate his developments of "the land ethic" and the need for an "ecological conscience." These developments were enmeshed with paradigmatic concepts of race science and its applications, which also took on various guises as one or another became more obviously repellent. Because Leopold's responses to the vexing question of how to get people to act better did not root out racist assumptions about *who* mattered, his models of good land use and how to achieve it would continue to privilege Euro-Americans in ownership of and access to land. And this raised a frustrating contradiction – a supremely capable people (according to themselves) whose success at building power was outpacing the development of their ethics. Leopold's view would continue to look straight past those who already had long records of intelligent, adaptive, successful land-keeping. Continuing on this path could be to continue suppressing many "practical models for ethics offered by many North American Indigenous persons," as Whyte discusses. For instance, as expressed in collective water-protection action of Anishinaabe women in the Great Lakes Basin, practical models that involve "people who are finding ways to live their responsibilities in contemporary times" and "in their own homelands, or in the territories to which they've been forcibly removed." The practical models already amalgamate Indigenous peoples' own relationships with water, wild rice, sturgeon, or caribou, ecologies and agricultures, scientific research, and "anti-colonial action," and "critical feedback-loops" (Whyte, 2024). Such ongoing suppression would run counter to stable Indigenous-settler coalitions.

A permutation of the vexing matter of how to get the people in power to use land better arises in openly racialized terms, within the first half of Leopold's career. For instance, it occurs in a 1922 talk "uncovered and submitted" by a colleague and first published in 1946 as a work standing the test of time and as a landmark on Southwestern U.S. erosion problems and proposed solutions.[59] Leopold begins, provocatively, by addressing his audience as members of "the Nordic race," a nineteenth- to twentieth-century self-mirroring classification of superior humans from the north of Europe (Powell, 2015: 201). Like many of his colleagues, it seems Leopold was familiar with the influential, purportedly scientific text *The Passing of the Great Race, or, The Racial Basis of European History* (1916) by conservationist, anthropologist, and eugenicist Madison

---

[59] Leopold, a thirteen-year veteran of the USFS, presented "Erosion As a Menace to the Social and Economic Future of the Southwest" to the meeting of the New Mexico Association for Science. As indicated in a footnote, Leopold's colleague H.H. Chapman "uncovered and submitted" Leopold's written talk to *The Journal of Forestry,* which Leopold had formerly served as associate editor.

Grant.[60] Fairfield Osborn, Sr., another influential conservationist and eugenicist who introduced the book, claimed that Grant had "turned this historical sketch into the current of a great biological movement," terming it "a hereditary history of Europe" (1). In the book, Grant describes Nordics as the human stock (particularly its Anglo-Saxon branch) upon which the U.S. must chiefly depend (3). "Anthropologists tell us," as Leopold framed a similar idea, "that we, the Nordics, have a racial genius for pioneering surpassing all other races and all other creatures in ability to reduce the wilderness to possession," from "Alaska to Brazil" and elsewhere. The reach of this "destiny of conquest and colonization" was wide and ongoing, "Leopold noted in his 1922 remarks" (1946b: 627).

And, then, a twist. Leopold had observed that Nordic methods clearly were successful in the sense of "conquering the wilderness." They had not been so "efficient"; however, he prodded his audience, in "creating more useful land with the labor of our hands than we are unintentionally destroying with the trampling of our feet." "We, the community, are the fools and it is high time we realized it and mended our ways," Leopold urged. He went on to diagnose, in detail, "the direct result of our own mis-use of the country we are trying to improve" (627). Overgrazing livestock, he explained, created flooding that ate away the soil, which was the foundation for the range industry, sustained family ranching, and, in particular, of the local Blue River community. The land and infrastructures would be expensive to replace, if they even could be. This, Leopold stressed, again, ironically, "is Nordic genius." "It sounds more like what John Burroughs said about the genius of the potato bug," he continued, "which, by exterminating the potato, thereby exterminates itself" (629).

Included as snapshots of destruction, Leopold describes "ancient fruit trees" rooted in cliffs of clay suddenly toppling "into the man-made abyss" created by Euro-settler overuse – "the symbol," Leopold says, of "a fruitful land reverting to the aboriginal desert." And he reports that, in "Navajo country," geologists discovered underground water recently exposed by erosion (presumably also due to overgrazing) now open to evaporation, and, thus, to further loss (630). Leopold here passes over opportunities for respecting the skills and ethics of past Indigenous land users and the constraints placed on current ones. He jumps over them to propose his own remedies to better settler land uses. "Nobody advocates that we cease grazing," Leopold stresses. "That would be a merely negative solution;" he explains, "a confession of impotence and lack of skill" (631).

Characteristically, Leopold proposes his own positive remedies. In the case of erosion in the U.S. Southwest, he considers a proper balance between public

---

[60] Leopold donated $5 to honor Madison Grant with a note saying: "I have long admired his [Grant's] work and have read his publications with great interest" (Letter to Mr. W. Redmond Cross, December 15, 1930: LP 9/25/10-2 2[1]: 15–16).

and private responsibility. Public agencies, he suggests, could help develop supportive technologies and lend a hand in performing work on rivers and reservoirs. The bulk of the "control work," however, to "minimize ill effects of grazing" must be done by "the land owner," Leopold says. "The day will come," he urges, "when the ownership of land will carry with it the obligation to use and protect it from erosion so that it is not a menace to other landowners and the public" (631). In this case, in the matter of his audience living up to their superior status, he foresees a future in which law-enforced landowner responsibility is in place. Until the day when better land care becomes legally normalized, however, Leopold offers tips for short-term techniques of prevention and cure – such as fencing, stream-bank restoration, cattle watering, flood diversion methods, and gully control. Several measures would take coordinated, neighborly efforts. Leopold here calls in to action and privilege a more select subset of "Nordics" – "those owners sufficiently progressive, or sufficiently menaced by impending loss" by erosion (631), thus undermining land's "ultimate capacity for supporting man" (633). Given the urgency to protect the public interest in habitable land, Leopold also recommends government power to inspect all lands "as to the adequacy of erosion control," with authority to "force all owners, whether private or public, to conserve their lands or pass title to someone who will" (633).

Leopold, well-respected by his scientific audiences, had the confidence and rapport to issue such firm recommendations. The framing of his argument in openly racialized and discriminatory terms with a rhetorical tone that was provocatively ironic and even self-mocking indicates his authority. The model of his future vision expanded from a select "progressive" minority of the already elite "blue-eyed pioneers" (627). It expressed hope in the day when the values of that minority, one way or another, would live up to their public obligations as settled landowning citizens. Side-by-side with Leopold's frustration over the ways his powerful "race" were misusing land, his focus on their own self-improvement would remain steadfast. At this elitist, racialized and racist intersection of frustration over settler-colonial land ruination, in other words, Leopold would continue to marginalize Indigenous, Black and other groups who were not legible as the "someone who will" control erosion, but, at the most, as the someone who, perhaps in the past, had existed as conservative, if not intelligent, land users.

Leopold's provocative use of the racial category "Nordic" in "Erosion as a Menace" could also have been a wink at outdated terminology, albeit not race/ism itself, with a nod to changing scientific understandings. Whether taken at face value or as ironic, Leopold's language, rhetorically, could support a shared, even clubby sense of superiority he could then challenge his learned audiences to live up to.[61] During the twentieth century, many scientists were finding biological race categories irresolvable. Many were backing away from scientific racism, popularized from the 1850s on, and heading toward general agreement that race is socially constructed (Tallbear, 2013: 33, 37; Powell, 2016: 159). A few years before Grant's book, anthropologist Franz Boas had published *The Mind of Primitive Man* (1911). A "Boasian model" had been gaining traction around the turn of the twentieth century. This, too, was helping shift racial conceptualization away from a Social Darwinist "survival of the fittest," evolutionary march of progress – with its view of Europeans races outcompeting all others – and toward a view of plural "cultures." Yet "cultures" outfitted the race concept with new clothes. The Boasian model, on the surface, seemed a move away from racism while keeping racialized white settler-colonial power structures intact, which continued to disappear Indigenous Peoples (Tallbear, 2013: 36; Simpson, 2018: 178; McLean, 2020). "Indians," since the "influx of the more numerous Europeans," Boas wrote, have never become an "important element in *our* population" (Simpson, 2018: 176). Boas's model, however, neglected the surrounding context of "geographic formalization of the settler status of the nation-state with its attendant race-based 'immigration,'" in the words of political anthropologist Audra Simpson, through appropriation of Indigenous lands and relegation of Indigenous Peoples to various elsewheres (2018: 171).

Boas was not part of Leopold's scientific and conservation communities like Grant was. I don't find direct reference to Boas in Leopold's works or letters. Yet there is a seemingly reverberant echo of language in Leopold's "Some Fundamentals of Conservation in the Southwest" (1923). This essay, unpublished until 1979, appeared in the first volume of *Environmental Ethics* as "Leopold's first attempt to deal with the moral aspects of conservation and develop a philosophy of conservation" (131).[62] As in "Erosion As a Menace," Leopold describes his frustration with dry farming, which is "slicing at one end of our loaf while the other end sloughs away in waste" until they meet in the middle and it becomes clear "the whole loaf" was needed (Flader and Callicott, 1991: 87). "Erosion eats into our hills like a contagion, and floods bring down loosened soil upon our valleys like a scourge," he wrote in a prophetic tone. "Water, soil, animals, and plants – the very fabric of prosperity – react to destroy each other and us." "Science can and must unravel those reactions," he

---

[61] Powell (2015) takes Leopold's use of "Nordic" at face value, arguing how Leopold's racism, pertaining to pioneers in the wilderness, perpetuated exclusion of people racialized as non-white from the U.S. environmental movement. Meine (2022) takes Leopold's use of "Nordic" ironically and as evidence that Leopold "was no admirer of eugenicist ideology."

[62] The essay is followed by commentary by Leopold biographer Susan Flader and has been popularized and central in the work of Leopoldian philosopher J. Baird Callicott. It was published posthumously with permission of Leopold's family.

continued, "and government must enforce the findings of science." Expanding from the legal and top-down emphasis of "Erosion as a Menace," Leopold here points to "the economic bearing of conservation on the future of the Southwest" (93) before moving from conservation "as an economic issue"[63] to consider its "moral aspects" (94) in a section titled "Conservation as a Moral Issue."

In this concluding section, Leopold travels from the Judeo-Christian book of Ezekiel to the Russian philosopher Peter Ouspensky to the Scottish-American wilderness preservationist John Muir to the American poet William Cullen Bryant to the Australian philosopher John Hadley to "God himself." He evokes scientific understandings of and intuitive respect for earth's interdependency, responsibility to future generations, care for waterways and a living earth, and religious humility regarding the role of "man" in creation. Since, to Leopold's perspective, "most of mankind today" profess religious and/or scientific anthropomorphism, he rhetorically grants "the earth is for man." Then he raises a question: "What man?" "Five races – five cultures – have flourished here," he writes. Though he lists only four –"cliff dwellers," "the Pueblos," "the Spaniards," "and now we Americans." He argues that "We may truthfully say of our four predecessors that they left the earth alive, undamaged."[64]

While exchanging "we, the Nordics" for "we Americans," a term for those with political control that might sound both less racist and more assimilative, this summary speeds past invasion and colonization, treaty-breaking, the discontinuation of treaty-making, genocide, enslavement, incarceration (including boarding schools), revolution, ongoing Indigenous resistance, and land annexation and dispossession of Pueblo, Ute, Apache, and other Indigenous Tribes and communities. It recognizes neither Black persons such as the nearby Buffalo soldiers nor dispossessed Mexican Americans, overlooking, in the words of Queer Chicana scholar Priscilla Ybarra, "generations of [Mexican Americans'] experience with the land" (2016: 5). "Hidden in plain sight," Ybarra says, in fact, was the "Mexican American background" of Leopold's own wife, Estella Bergere Leopold, and their five children as well as Estella's family's inheritance of land through dispossession of Pueblo Tribes (2022: 31–32).[65]

---

[63] Environmental scholar Qi Feng Lin writes about Leopold's economics thinking.

[64] Leopold's argument for keeping a Puebloan "fragment" was set in the context of the inevitability, in his words, of "the [Pueblo] Indian culture and ours" being "placed in competition for the possession of this country" (Flader and Callicott, 1991: 102). It is worth reflecting on this narrative, too, in possible relation to Leopold's rising view of land "as an energy circuit" upon which population scientists of the 1920s were suggesting evolution worked to select incipient, self-organizing systems that maximized fluxes and/or efficiency (Warren, 2016: 190).

[65] Also an online version: Ybarra, P. (2022). "The Forgotten History of Wilderness, and a Possible Future," www.hcn.org/articles/books-wilderness-is-stolen-land.

On the other hand, Leopold's moral narrative does conclude with wondering what the sixth "race" or "culture" "shall say about us." He thus acknowledges, with humility, that no civilization lasts forever, including his own self-impressed one, while goading readers toward the matter that keeps vexing him. Leopold asks rhetorically, "if there be, indeed, a special nobility inherent in the human race – a special cosmic value, distinctive from and superior to all other life – by what token shall it be manifest?" He follows this question with two alternatives and ends with a final assertion: "By a society decently respectful of its own and all other life, capable of inhabiting the earth without defiling it?" "Or," he continues, echoing "Erosion as a Menace," by a society like that of John Burroughs potato bug, which exterminated the potato, and thereby exterminated itself? As one or the other," Leopold concludes, "we shall be judged [in the words of Robert Louis Stevenson] in 'the derisive silence of eternity'" (Flader and Callicott, 1991: 96–97).

Leopold's terms shift swiftly – "races" or "cultures," "we Americans," "we," "the human race" – but the undercurrent remains constant. The troubling question remains – how shall Euro-American settler colonizers prove their mettle as good land owners? The trouble goes hand in hand with Indigenous elimination and land dispossession. What was to be done, given the paradoxical assumptions that those in power were racially and/or culturally advanced? Here is a people recently claiming the highest order evolutionary capacity to control nature rather than be controlled by it (Tallbear, 2013: 36), or to be the more "sturdy" (Simpson, 2018: 175) or competitive "culture" (Flader and Callicott, 1991: 102). Yet the same people lack the self-control and skills of positive land use. Below the surface, Leopold's diagnoses and remedies repeatedly leave racist structures intact. He questions many things, but he does not reflect on the histories of "*our* four predecessors," in his terms, as skilled thinkers and inventors who "left the earth alive, undamaged" (Flader and Callicott, 1991: 96). He does not consider the wherewithal of those hidden in plain sight. Leopold might have been willing, even courageously so, to grill the "nobility" of his own powerful society. Nonetheless, in various ways, his narratives continue suppressing Indigenous presence. Doing the opposite would be to moot the very framing of the frustrating contradiction. Leopold's narratives would head, from here on, toward grappling with conservation as a moral issue, toward the development of his land ethic, toward the goal of "improving ourselves" which would be to "make functional" or "evolve" "an ecological conscience" (Flader and Callicott, 1991: 340, 345) among private land owners who were predominantly male and white.

There is another loaf-wasting story of U.S. land possession that did not surface as a concern in Leopold's historical and contemporary narratives, nor in *Aldo Leopold's Odyssey*, except, again, in pioneering terms. There were the violent U.S. appropriations and exchanges of the Indigenous territories west of the Mississippi and the forced relegations there of eastern Tribes, as their homelands were taken. Euro-American settler colonialist boundary-making expressed rapacity for land. It, too, expressed a habit of taking more than giving, which would undercut themselves. As the U.S. sliced westward from the Atlantic the possibility of more land sloughed away upon reaching the Pacific.[66] As settlers re-surged eastward somewhere in the middle they met the front from the west. And, as discussed by Australian historian and scholar Patrick Wolfe: "There was simply no space left for [Indian] removal." Indigenous people who were now "contained within Euroamerican society" became subject to a rising force of U.S. strategies for Indigenous elimination by assimilation (2006: 399).

This story has been overshadowed in U.S. education and in Leopoldian narratives by the pioneering terms of American historian Frederick Jackson Turner, who coincidentally became Leopold's near neighbor in Wisconsin. As I summarized in *Aldo Leopold's Odyssey*, Turner proposed that the challenges of frontier life, of clearing forests and cultivating crops, had forged citizens of self-reliance and fortitude, a new national type, the democratic self-made man, free and equal (Warren, 2016: 21–22). Writing in the 1890s, Turner had declared the U.S. frontier was closed, the "vacant spaces" filled up, "a people thrown back upon itself." "Its diverse elements," Turner proposed, "are being fused into national unity" (Warren: 36–7, 102). It seemed to Turner that a shift from pioneering to the formation of a permanent civilization was taking place. For Leopold's part, as a scientific forester and, later, as an academic land ecologist, he had taken leads in counseling U.S. citizens to remedy the wood and game shortages, soil erosion, flooding, and losses of "wild things" left in the wake of pioneering and to do better. Yet, even for Leopold, "'nationalism' in its best sense," would continue hearkening back to Euro-American pioneers' "cultural inheritance" (1949: 188). Among the "cultural values" of wildlife, of "the sports, customs, and experiences that renew contacts with wild things," as he would write in his *Almanac*, was the "split-rail value." This value encompassed "any experience that reminds us of our distinctive national origins and evolution." This was exemplified by "a boy scout [who] has tanned a coonskin cap, and goes Daniel-Booneing in the willow thicket below the tracts." "He is reenacting American history." And, "to that extent," is "culturally prepared to face the dark and bloody realities of the present" (1949: 177).

---

[66] In other terms, in 1925, Leopold suggested that "we have come to the end of our pioneer environment and are about to push its remnants into the Pacific" (Flader and Callicott, 1991: 137).

"Daniel-Booneing" would be, "to that extent," a re-enactment of violent appropriation of Tsalaguwetiyi (Cherokee, East), S'atsoyaha (Yuchi), and Shawandasse Tula (Shawanwaki/Shawnee) territories, brought into Kentucky statehood, as well as of hunting skills and various woodcrafts, in heroic terms, second to none, including Indigenous ones. "Dark and bloody," according to the Kentucky Heritage Council,[67] gestures to a belief that these Indigenous sovereignties had hunted and fought over the land, but had never lived permanently anywhere in the Commonwealth – a well-practiced excuse for Euro-American taking. "Daniel-Booneing" would be to model, in play-clothes, how settler colonialism "destroys to replace," as Wolfe discusses referencing strategies of U.S.-supported Zionism against Palestinian existence. Allusions such as these call for further exploration (beyond Leopold), both in terms of how they apply to Indigenous persons and to structural, if not consciously intentional, nationalistic schemes of demolition-to-remake the fruitfulness of the land as a whole (Wolfe, 2006: 388). They remind how destruction – as an intention in itself – to various degrees and kinds, belongs to settler colonialism. They point to how "being fused into national unity" may not be a shift from pioneering, but a platform along a continuous, ongoing "structural genocide," to apply Wolfe's term (403). Such awareness might help in getting to the roots of Leopold's and many settlers' ongoing passionate frustrations over why none of our environmental or conservation movements, to date, have been successful in staving off continuous, ongoing land misuse in the U.S. (and beyond).

With regard to fusing national unity, in Turner's terms, or, in other words, to addressing an "expansion-conservation tension" in the U.S., I surveyed three historical ideas in *Aldo Leopold's Odyssey*: buying more land to keep the frontier open, which appeared finished; "reclaiming" new farms by irrigating more drylands (without the wastage Leopold railed against); and applying scientific methods to enhance intergenerational sustainability of renewable resources, including forests, ranges, and fisheries (Warren, 2016: 37–38). I left out how U.S. strategies to eliminate Indigenous Peoples also turned inwards to "the individual Indian below [the tribal surface]," in Wolfe's words (2006: 399). In the late 1800s, strategies increasingly featured measures for breaking down Tribes and assimilating Native persons and their tribal lands into "White society" (400).

This process became apparent in 1871 when the U.S. discontinued treaty-making. A central tactic was the Dawes Severalty Act of 1887, which broke

---

[67] Kentucky Heritage Council. "The Myth of Kentucky as a 'Dark and Bloody Ground,'" https://heritage.ky.gov/Documents/Myth%20of%20Dark%20and%20Bloody%20Ground.pdf.

tribal land into individual allotments to ostensibly turn Indigenous persons into private landowners on the path to the American Dream (Wolfe, 2006: 400; Simpson 2018: 171). In effect, Indigenous numbers plummeted to their lowest recorded levels. Recent scholars estimate that in 1492 there were some eighteen million persons, or, very roughly five persons per square mile. This was greater than the human density of Leopold's Southwest district during his whole tenure. By the turn of the nineteenth century, Indigenous persons numbered approximately 228,000, averaging fewer than one person per square mile (Dunbar-Ortiz, 2014: 136–138; Gilio-Whitaker, 2019: 49). And, as Wolfe notes, land transference to settlers sky-rocketed. Between 1881 and 1931, total U.S. acreage in Indigenous hands fell by two thirds, from approximately 155 million to 52 million acres (Wolfe, 2006: 400), while Native Americans, overall, had a marked "demographic explosion" in the twentieth century (Tallbear, 2013: 46). Meanwhile, under both the Dawes Act and the 1934 Indian Reform Act (which allowed a brief swell in tribal lands), the U.S. government deployed blood quantum requirements that, in effect, were to continue a process of racialized assimilation (Wolfe, 2006: 400; Ben-zvi, 2007: 226; Tallbear, 2013: 460; Taffa, 2024: 70) that also continued intersecting with race science (Turda, 2012: 70–71; Tallbear 2013: 48).

Remaining buried within Leopold's models of human ethics is this ruthless process of transference of lands from Indigenous to white people while devaluing Indigenous social and political norms and elevating settler ones, including the institution of private property.[68] Integrated within Leopold's racist models for addressing the troubling question of how white landowners would become better land users is a history of ideas about population control, scientific and ideological. Even as Indigenous numbers fell and settler numbers rose, the fear of Euro-American white race deterioration, if not outright extinction, detailed in Grant's 1916 book, did not disappear. From the late nineteenth century, white settlers worried that Black persons and other non-white people, including incoming immigrants, would out-reproduce them (Powell, 2015: 222). "Fear of human extinction has been the drum beaten by every prophet from St. John to the Los Angeles cults," Leopold claimed in a 1941 classroom lecture (Flader and Callicott, 1991: 281). On the other hand, through the twentieth century, national to global overpopulation became of increasing concern in the U.S. In the same 1941 lecture, "Ecology and Politics," Leopold stressed the importance of ecological limits, including on human population densities. By the 1940s, with another world war looming, that question of how technologically advanced

---

[68] Writings of legal scholar Eric Freyfogle feature Leopold's ideas in relation with private property. My harmful experience with this person as a former graduate advisor has already been noted.

U.S. Euro-Americans could improve their ethics overlapped with how to keep their own, not to mention global numbers, within lands' carrying capacities.

At the foundation of the ecological concept of carrying capacity is a theory of English economist, cleric, and scholar Thomas Malthus (1766–1834). In 1798, Malthus published his first edition of *An Essay on the Principle of Population*. His argument centered scarcity and competition. He suggested that population growth was exponential and would outgrow the arithmetical increase of food supply upon which human persons and other animals depended. Thus ever looming, as well as explaining the England around him, were "misery and vice," acting as checks on endless numeric expansion. In a field influenced by Malthusian ideas, Leopold's research related to preventing overgrazed ranges and increasing game (contra the protectionist view of his former mentor Hornaday) became focused on animal population numbers in relation to their food supply and also other "environmental factors," such as predation, hunting, and disease. The control of population density, by diagnosing and manipulating various "factors of productivity," was the work of the game manager, and this work could also apply to human density, Leopold proposed in his path-breaking 1933 textbook *Game Management* (25, 39, 41, 423).

That human beings were subject to the same forces as other animals was a view Leopold shared. This suggested analogies.[69] At the same time, to the degree of their advancement, at least some humans also differed from other animals by merit of technologies for increasing food supply that could support more people and/or more game, at least to the limit of lands' carrying capacities. In *Game Management,* Leopold defined carrying capacity, hearkening to Malthus, as the "maximum density" a particular range was "capable of supporting" (1933: 50–51, 395; Warren 2016: Chapter 4). There was some evidence of other ecological patterns, too. Bobwhite, a game bird of brushy meadows, for example, were subject not only to carrying capacity but also seemed to exhibit a scientific "phenomenon called 'Saturation Point.'" According to Leopold, this self-limiting feature appeared to inhere in some species keeping "social units" from exceeding a fixed number per "unit area" (49; see also Callicott and Freyfogle, 1999: 134–135).

Leopold, underscoring human-animal commonalities, offered one "little analogue with humans" of Bobwhites. "Man thinks of himself as not subject to any density limit," Leopold said. "Industrialism, imperialism, and that whole array of population behaviors," he argued, were manifestations of "the 'bigger and better' ideology" and the "Mosaic injunction" to fill up the earth. That is,

---

[69] Powell (2015) discusses some of these analogies in relation to his argument that Leopod's wilderness ideas were connected with Malthusian ones.

"slums, wars, birth-controls, and depressions," he continued, "may be construed as ecological symptoms that our assumption about human density limits is unwarranted" (see also Flader and Callicott, 1991: 283). Thus "the lowly bobwhite" had a "lesson in sociology" to teach human beings. The Bobwhite, Leopold said, "'refuses,'" in biological terms, "to live in slums, and concentrates his racial effort on quality, not ciphers." Occasionally, "his racial exuberance," in other words, Bobwhites' persistent reproductive force, "gets the upper hand," Leopold explained. The consequences included economic and social unrest – "Bobwhite's natural monogamy breaks down," he said, in sexually moralizing terms – and Bobwhite "civilization relapses to near-zero for a new start" (1933: 49).

Leopold concluded this analogy by observing that the Bobwhites' "environmental and racial tolerances" reveal the birds to be "as finicky as any bluestocking." While both anthropomorphizing and taking a swing at intellectual women, this was to underscore the ill effects of what he deemed too-intensive management. This included game farming, which produced mob-like or artificialized populations, to his observation, which also imply interspecies supremacy, crediting as little agency to birds and bugs as to lower i.e., Indigenous humans. With another jab at his own heritage, Leopold pointed to the ill consequences if game farmers "planted the wrong race" in the wrong place, presumably referring to moving Bobwhites into new habitats. He left his phrasing ambiguous enough, though, for "the Nordics to ponder." This draws attention, again, to another version of that unrelentingly vexing matter, a "paradox" of Euro-American technological power overwhelming ethics in land use (1933: 422). Leopold's suggestions in *Game Management* included to not waste the likely fleeting advantage of "our relatively low human population density as compared with Europe"[70] (394), which offered a chance to avoid "slum" conditions for both Bobwhites and Euro-American land owners.

The opportunity of relatively low human density, Leopold wrote, "raises the interesting question of whether, having automatically filled up the biological niche which Columbus found for us, we will prove capable of regulating our future human population density by some qualitative standard" (1933: 395). One such standard was "natural beauty" (422), he thought, versus subjecting ourselves (like Burroughs's potato bug and/or over-farmed game birds) to the

---

[70] Leopold's comparisons of the United States with Europe has been well-noted yet perhaps underappreciated. It is well documented throughout Leopold scholarship that his thinking was influenced in many ways by his 1935 stay in Germany, sponsored by the Oberlaender Trust. With the rising Third Reich, strong supporters of both nature conservation and human eugenics, it could be enlightening to apply the frameworks of this Element or others informed by more critical lenses (e.g., anti-fascist ones) in revisiting his complexly stimulating trip and in exploring its upshots, which I am unable to cover here.

otherwise deleterious consequences. To "prove capable," Leopold proposed, "the task of the future is to learn how to live with our inventions" as a matter of "a new conviction" (420). The task, in other words, was to bring about "a new attitude toward the land" (420), in the "average citizen," which incorporated the "conviction" that the "capacity to live in high density without befouling and denuding his environment, rather than such density, is the true test of whether he is civilized" (423). What was needed, Leopold thought, was the transformation of the still small minority ready to resist the ugliness of "economic determinism" and its "food factories," "developing a culture" of land possessors that would be "morally and intellectually" keeping pace with the consequences of its own innovativeness (422–423).

Many of Leopold's evidence-based and moral understandings changed and developed over his career, while white supremacy remained rooted and continued to take new forms, often clothed in science. In the 1941 lecture, "Ecology and Politics," and maintaining Malthusian-based population terms, Leopold defined "carrying capacity" for his students. "Every environment carries not only characteristic kinds of animals, but characteristic *numbers* of each." "Thus," he proposed, "the characteristic number of Indians in virgin America was small." "More Indians," he continued, "would either have starved or killed each other off; fewer Indians would have risked annihilation of the race in some blizzard, drouth, or epidemic" (Flader and Callicott, 1991: 282). According to this scenario, if Indigenous Peoples had "left the earth alive," as he had put it in his 1923 "Some Fundamentals" (Flader and Callicott, 1991: 96), it had not been intentional but rather analogous with a Bobwhite-like inherence within their "races" or "cultures."

"When we arrived on the scene," Euro-Americans, on the other hand, had "raised the carrying capacity of the land for man by means of tools," Leopold told his students (282). Stressing yet again the vexing paradox in new terms, he proposed that increasing "take" from the land without reciprocal "give" would not be sustainable (282). "All ecology is replete with laws," Leopold explained, "which begin to operate at a threshold, and cease operating at a ceiling" (284). Or, as he would discuss in his *Almanac*, land use, including human population density, needed to be tooled to the differing resiliencies of each place. Western Europe, under pressure, was "tough" and "elastic," he thought, as was, perhaps, Japan. "Most other civilized regions," Leopold wrote, were in "various stages of [ecological] disorganization" and wastage, reducing carrying capacity while exceeding it (1949: 219). For example, "already subsisting on exploitative agriculture," Leopold wrote, "Most of South America is overpopulated in this sense" (219). "Ecology knows of no density relationship that holds for indefinitely wide limits," he urged (220). How, then, could conservation support not just the land's, but the attendant human capacity for thoughtful, land-use competence (1933: 422), which he had continued believing was so scarce? How could wildlife managers and other conservationists bring ethics into sync with the world-wide expansion of powerful "technological culture" (Flader and Callicott, 1991: 285)? Yet, across time and space and various scenarios, while deeply frustrated by members of his own Euro-American citizenry, he excluded Indigenous people and others racialized as non-white as having no capacity for intentional inventiveness in technology or philosophy.

"We assume," Leopold said, "that increasing 'take' (i.e., more extraction, conversion, and consumption of resources) always raises standards of living." "Sometimes it merely raises population levels," he argued in his 1941 lecture (Flader and Callicott, 1991: 285). He explained this to his students with another animal analogy. If you feed starving deer, he said, they reproduce more, over-browse, and damage their range more. Left without the land's support, the deer themselves deteriorate, Leopold said. If "Indians" held within U.S. bounds seem to be like Bobwhites, "South African natives," as Leopold proposed, were like deer (presumably without a built-in saturation point). In contrast, the !Xam (San) of southern Africa say of themselves: "Our strong spirit is not loud" and call for quiet listening.[71] San tell their own story that white colonizers believed "a dead bushman was better" and hunted them down to be shot like dogs. By 1950, all San communities had been destroyed or dispossessed, including expelled from a new national park. British and Boer colonizers, imposing wide swaths of ill-fitting agriculture, pushed San survivors to become "squatters," marginalized within their own homelands by hostile Euro-settlers.[72] Whereas, the story Leopold told was that the British "ameliorated" the "hard lot of South African natives (by medical service, better farming, etc.)" resulting in increased population numbers without improvement in living conditions.[73] "Perhaps only animals capable of qualitative self-improvement and quantitative self-limitation can be safely ameliorated," Leopold concluded (285).

This was both a warning and an obviously racist comment endorsing genocidal consequences. It can also be read as a challenge to the select, young Euro-American audience he was educating. Weren't they the ones holding both superior intelligence and an ethics of self-limitation, or, at least – given the

---

[71] !Khwa ttu San Heritage Centre. "Hear it from the San," www.khwattu.org/heritage-centre-museum/.

[72] !Khwa ttu San Heritage Centre, "Edited from Tracks Across the Sands Hugh Brody," www.khwattu.org/heritage-centre-museum/.

[73] And, again, in 1946, as Leopold drafted further details on his land-health concept, he included medicine along with industrialization and "other devices" as factors possibly contributing to "the impending disorganization of land as taking over the reducing job after we foiled the normal mechanisms" (Callicott and Freyfogle, 1999: 225).

frustrating contradiction – the ones bearing technological prowess and access to land with the capacity for ethical advancement in support of tools and land use attunement? On the one hand, despite the cause-effect relationship between colonialist exploitation, reduced land capacity, and human suffering, Leopold had suggested *not* intervening while environmental factors did the job of limiting populations of suffering colonized peoples such as North American and southern African Indigenous Peoples who were racialized as non-white. On the other hand, frustrated with the majority of Euro-American settlers, Leopold's land ethic also would incorporate Malthusian-influenced contrivances, including qualitative self-improvement, to limit the population density of those racialized as white (e.g., Leopold, 1933; 1949: 220). Moreover, Leopold's proposals for human density control and human transformation coincided not only with scientific racism but also with the trending paradigm of eugenics.

Malthus's ideas about resource restraints on otherwise persistent forces of population growth had helped Charles Darwin bring together his theory of evolution by natural selection. Reading in Malthus of "a struggle for existence," Darwin devised the idea that "favorable variations" of plants and animals "would tend to be preserved," and "unfavorable" ones "destroyed," giving rise to new "species" (Seidl and Tisdell, 1999: 398). In the 1930s and 1940s, Darwinian natural selection blended with Mendelian genetics, giving rise to population genetics, wherein "population" became another guise for "race" (Tallbear, 38).[74] This new field of population genetics would study the genetic basis of evolution, including how natural selection changes the genetic composition of localized, interbreeding groups, including human ones.[75] Population genetics intersected with the older field of population ecology, which, as seen in Leopold's work, explored dynamics between environmental factors and population numbers. This field, fascinated with complex interrelations, was also rooted in Darwinian science. The foci of population ecologists included questions related to threats of extinction and future projections of survival, including of humans.

Meanwhile, since 1900, new developments in genetics also had been revolutionary in the development of eugenics (Turda, 2012: 69). Nineteenth-century English scientific scholar Herbert Spencer had coined the phrase "survival of the fittest" to conceptualize Darwinian evolution and applied it to human societies. Social Darwinists (pre-Boas) had considered "culture" (singular)

---

[74] "Population," like "species," also are processes of assumption-ridden differentiation, the boundary-making itself, a site of conflict (e.g., Wolfe, 2006: 408).

[75] *Stanford Encyclopedia of Philosophy*, "Population genetics," https://plato.stanford.edu/entries/population-genetics/

a higher evolutionary stage, characterized, in general, by superior human agency (Tallbear, 2013: 36). In 1883, Sir Francis Galton launched "eugenics" – from "eugenes" or "good stock" – as a Darwinian science applied to human societies. This field would be "equally applicable to men, brutes, and plants," Galton argued. Eugenics, he wrote, means "to express the science of improving stock, which is by no means confined to questions of judicious mating, but which, especially in the case of man, takes cognizance of all influences that tend in however remote a degree to give to the more suitable races or strains of blood a better chance of prevailing speedily over the less suitable than they otherwise would have had" (Galton, 1883: 17). The complexities contained within this definition are vast. The phrase, "of all influences," is one example. It bears, among others, the challenge of separating what Galton termed "nurture" – "acquired through education and circumstance" – and "nature" – "that which was in the original grain of his constitution" (128). Another example is the enfolding into "a better chance" of the possibilities of both negative and positive influences, respectively, those obstructing the continuance of "the less suitable" stock versus privileging the "more suitable races or strains of blood."

Evolutionary ornithologist and museum curator Richard Prum argues that, in one way or another, between the 1890s and 1940s "every professional geneticist and evolutionary biologist in the United States and Europe was either an ardent proponent of eugenics, a dedicated participant in eugenic social programs, or a happy fellow traveler. Full stop" (Prum, 2017: 326). Leopold touched on his sense of involvement in his 1941 lecture. "Ecology," he said, "is here only a bystander" to the rising, machine-made threat of "genetic deterioration of the human species." "Except in this sense," he continued: ecology "offers abundant testimony that only healthy species achieve continuity" (Flader and Callicott, 1991: 282). "There can be no doubt," Leopold told his students, "that better human stocks, both as to inheritance and environment, are more likely to find a *modus vivendi* than poorer ones" (286). Hand in hand with his support of negative proposals to manage human densities and his tendering of positive ones to enhance human capacities, Leopold's belief in better or worse human kinds – with both hereditary (nature) and environmental (nurture) facets – aligned with basic tenets of Galtonian eugenics, intersecting with both scientific racism and ableism. These facets of Leopold's narratives aligned, albeit often more cautiously, with the far more voluble paradigmatic formulations of prominent, dedicated contemporary eugenicists and/or environmental Malthusians within the large circle of his conservation colleagues.[76]

---

[76] Powell (2015) discusses the different receptions of Leopold's *Almanac* and two of his colleagues' books published around the same time in terms of overtness. Both Bill Vogt and Henry

These colleagues included Ellsworth Huntington, president of the American Eugenics Society (1934–38) and author of *Tomorrow's Children; The Goal of Eugenics* (1935), a rewrite of the "eugenics catechism." Huntington proposed that eugenics could correct "the present wrong kind of differential birthrate" (10) to "improve mankind" (7). He recommended negative policies to limit the birthrate among the worst and positive measures to increase it among the best, that is, "the native white population" (76). Huntington privileged rural family life, with conditions of health, childhood education, and economic opportunities, as matters important to nurturing the inheritance of desirable "innate capacities" (22), for example, intelligence, self-control, foresight, physical vigor. There was also New York Zoological Society president and Conservation Foundation co-founder, Henry Fairfield Osborn, Jr.[77] Even in the wake of "man's" wars, Osborn wrote in *Our Plundered Planet* (1948), "too many are left alive" (31) and high population density results in declines of persons' fitness (99). In a later work, Osborn supported the prevention of reproduction by those "who are mentally incompetent or physically defective" (Powell, 2015: 219). A third, fellow ecologist Bill Vogt, was among Leopold's closest colleagues. In Vogt's *The Road to Survival* (1948) a foundation of outspoken Malthusianism intersected with racism and eugenics. For instance, Vogt blamed U.S. colonialist measures to improve health and nutrition in Boriquén (aka Puerto Rico) for rising population accompanied by an ineffective birth control law and increasing misery in this "island slum." He recommended withholding global aid until the islanders adopted "a rational population policy" (1948: 77).[78] Linking socially objectionable traits with lineage (Powell, 2015:

Osborn, Jr's books, containing many blatant statements, had more divided reception and more immediate influence on public opinion. Leopold's book, on the other hand, was praised for its "thoughtful observations and poetic tone" and became "a near sacred text to environmentalists" (221–223). In my opinion, Leopold's rhetoric tended to be masterful. Overall, skill in keeping what is repellent under wraps, e.g., via complex thinking, ambiguity, in-group signalling and a gradient of forthrightness (often more so with intimates), can and does make discerning intention more challenging. Thus the repetition of the repellent – even if intention admits true caution and uncertainty – remains more likely.

[77] Powell (2015) discusses key similarities and differences between Osborn, Jr. and his father, Osborn, Sr. Both served the New York Zoological Society. The elder was an outspoken scientific racist and eugenicist. The younger considered a "reform eugenicist," "in the wake of Nazism," for palatability, shifting away from explicit connections of genetic fitness with race or class (220).

[78] Author Jamie Figueroa, Boricua (Afro-Taíno), by way of Ohio and a long-term resident of northern New Mexico, writes that "In the wake of Hurricane Maria [in 2017] . . . What might have been hidden from some could no longer be ignored, the neglect that killed Puerto Rican people, Boricuas, the abandonment of the island that is still a possession of the U.S. Cared for like an object, a thing, but not respected, not included, not equal." She quotes the former mayor of San Juan, Carmen Yulín Cruz Soto: "Because of racism, she explained, 'People . . . let others die because of who they were'" (2024: 209).

219), Vogt also thought that states should withhold support from "the senile, the incurables, the insane, the paupers and those who might be called ecological incompetents." Those who "expedite erosion" and otherwise deteriorate land, Vogt said, were "worse than paupers." They were "ecological Typhoid Marys," infecting everyone with "environmental sickness," whose government subsidized businesses must be "liquidated, at least in part" in the interest of "national survival." Hurting many in the short run, Vogt proposed, was necessary to prevent more suffering in the future (1948: 145).

Such perspectives obviously bypass social-structural analyses that incorporate justice. They circumvent access to hosts of valuable teachings related to "exploring and creating new ways of doing things that go beyond able-bodied /minded normativity," as creative and disability organizer Patricia Berne says (2015). These include how "disabled lands" as well as disabled persons "still dream," in the words of Russian-born NYC-based ecoartist and disability culture activist Marina Tsaplina.[79] Leopold valorizes land health, taking wilderness and the lands of Northwestern Europe as standards, the latter – co-constituted with its superior people – as "resistant to strain" (Leopold, 1949: 219) and possessing "extraordinary recuperative capacity" (Flader and Callicott, 1991: 213). In contrast, he marks down less "tough" lands, which, when abused become "deteriorated" and "despoiled," "mutilated," "sick," "deranged" or "wastage" (Leopold, 1946: 277; Callicott and Freyfogle, 1999: 172, 219; Leopold, 1949: 219). Similarly, he categorizes the frustrating majority of racialized white Americans as "average," mob-like on "stampede," and "mass-minded" in contrast with the minority who are "progressive," have mental capacity to "see" (at least some) ecological causes and effects, are physically healthy and personally cooperative, and value "primitive arts of wilderness travel" with the conscience to apply "voluntary adherence to an ethical code" (Flader and Callicott, 1991; Leopold 1946a: 279; Warren, 2016: 276; Leopold, 1949: 193–194, 177–178). This divide between seemingly ideal versus imperfect bodies/conditions can disrespect how valuable are traumatized or even just seemingly ordinary lands and persons, as themselves, who hold one another together – right now – in a world of just and "collective liberation ... where no body/mind is left behind."[80]

The consensus among scientists is more than a loose association. Huntington, Osborn, Jr., and Vogt and Leopold, to various degrees, expressed mutual

---

[79] Tsaplina, M. (2021). "Animate Earth," https://orionmagazine.org/article/the-animate-earth/.
[80] Berne, P. (2015). "Disability Justice: A Working Draft by Patty Berne," www.sinsinvalid.org/blog/disability-justice-a-working-draft-by-patty-berne; Ortiz, N. (2023). "Crip Ecologies," www.poetryfoundation.org/poetrymagazine/articles/157104/crip-ecologies-complicate-the-conversation-to-reclaim-power

appreciation for one another's contributions.[81] The ideas of Leopold and Vogt, in particular, often tracked with one another (Powell, 2015: 218; Warren, 2016: 168 fn 95; 249 fn 37; 254 fn64; Meine, 495, 523–525).[82] For instance, Leopold praised Vogt's book as based richly on examining animal analogies for solving "the world's human populations problems." He praised it as "the last work on conservation as applied to the world-wide problem of men and land" (1948).[83] Leopold may have been more skillful with rhetoric, more cautious, and, as he

---

[81] Vogt and Leopold served as advisors for the Conservation Foundation, which Fairfield Osborn, Jr. cofounded. In a letter to Osborn (April 1, 1948), Leopold looks forward to reading an inscribed copy of *The Plundered Planet*, which Osborn hopes he likes (letter, March 16, 1948). "I also read, with strong approval," Leopold said, your article in *The Atlantic,*" which contained many of the book's themes (LP 9/25/10-1: 2[10]: 805–806; Osborn, F. [1948]. "Crowded Off the Earth," https://cdn.theatlantic.com/media/archives/1948/03/181-3/132325215.pdf). Huntington's *The Pulse of Asia*, which proposed "a single consistent geographic theory of history" (14), influenced Leopold, who cited it in his 1920 "The Forestry of the Prophets" (Flader and Callicott, 1991: 73). Leopold and Huntington were acquainted at the 1931 Matamek Conference on Biological Cycles. Huntington's work was central and Leopold was greatly affected by the gathering (Warren, 2016: 117–123). When Vogt's publisher asked Leopold to comment on *Road to Survival*, Leopold responded that, though he had not seen it, he had otherwise "followed his thoughts with intense interest" and "bet it will have a large sale" (Warren 417-18 fn 64). Vogt also praised Leopold in *Road to Survival* (95) and, just before his death, Leopold included Vogt in a list of trusted reviewers of the essays that would become *A Sand County Almanac* (Meine, 2010: 523). As noted elsewhere (Meine, 497 and Powell, 218), after meeting with Osborn, Vogt, and the other advisors developing the new Conservation Foundation, Leopold praised "the outfit" to his son Starker, noting that "Bill [Vogt] and I found ourselves giving identical views, even tho [sic] we had hardly seen each other for years" (LP 10-1, 2 in Meine, 2010: 495; Powell, 2015: 218). Also showing what a circle-of-support there was, Osborn, in *Our Plundered Planet*, also thanked both Leopold and Vogt for the influences of their philosophical approaches (204). Both Vogt (xvi) and Osborn (after Leopold's passing, in his 1954 work, 228) also thanked Robert C. Cook, geneticist, demographer, and editor of *Journal of Heredity*, which, in 1946, reprinted Leopold's 1933 "The Conservation Ethic" as "Racial Wisdom and Conservation."

[82] In *The Road to Survival* there are many likenesses with Leopold in fundamental ecological conceptions, including carrying capacity (Vogt, 1948: 16, 91–93); in analogies between "primitive man ... the Indians of the United States" and "bobwhites" (40) or other "lower animals" (93); in relations of environment, racism, and population – there was the "inestimable advantage [in view of "racial survival] of a high death rate that kept down his population" thus keeping "plant cover ... little disturbed" (94); in demeaning the intelligence capacity of Indigenous (and racialized "Black" people) – the "African native" as "profoundly ignorant of the biology of his cattle as of his environment" (262), between deer overpopulation and "the human animal" (89, citing Leopold); and regarding the vexing contradiction, the challenge to "modern European man" (i.e., colonizers) not to be deer-like, but rather to engage their higher-brains in deciding "whether or not to make use of his special abilities," i.e., their advanced intelligence and technology (95–96) to survive rather than to destroy his own "tribe" (193); and in also observing the "cultural value of primitive tracts" (109).

[83] Leopold. (March 2, 1948). Letter to Mr. H.P. Swanson, William Sloane Assoc Publishers. In the back-and-forth correspondence with Swanson, who was happy to hear such high and authoritative praise on Vogt's book (March 4, 1948), Leopold acknowledged he had not yet seen Vogt's book. But, Leopold wrote, "I have followed his thoughts with intense interest" and "had no hesitancy whatever in expressing my appraisal of the forthcoming volume" (March 9, 1948; letter series in LP 9/25/10-1: 3[8]: 546–551).

aged, less certain about most things than many of his colleagues.[84] At the same, throughout his career, there is evidence that Leopold had been developing, in tandem with his land ethic and land health concepts, an ecological-evolutionary model of social change. It appears woven with certain threads of fixed, oppressive assumptions of settler colonial white supremacy, intersecting with environmental Malthusianism and eugenics, into the background of his ecological work.

Leopold's ecology was a genetics-adjacent model rooted in Darwinian science in support of healthy land and a "healthy [human] species." In light of the vexing contradiction, the "abundant testimony" of ecology pointed to the need for a land ethic to promote land health and to the need for "an ecological conscience" to carry it. Although sometimes admitting his forlorn hope, Leopold was not one to quit trying (Warren, 2016: 255). His model of human change takes up many possibilities. And it seems to manifest in at least two ways at once. On the one hand, encouraging "the love of nature" is an inclusive, tender venture; "ideas are evolving" (Flader and Callicott, 1991: 190) and "cultural values" and "ethics" are philosophical abstractions that thus can be altered by choice; ecology is research and wonder, laws are just, and the effects of economic carrots and sticks are just that, economic. On the other hand, Leopold evokes a murkier, nonetheless dynamic social-scientific framework that is racialized, as well as patriarchal, elitist and ableist, with not only environmental (nurture) components but also hereditary (nature) elements.

In these murkier depths, U.S. land owners had become mostly male and white. Leopold was facing the vexing contradiction of run-away technologies mutually deteriorating land and land's human inhabitants, increasingly worrisome (e.g., Flader and Callicott, 1991: 184; Leopold 1946a: 277; Freyfogle and Callicott, 1999: 172). Conservation policies could prevent not only erosion and other land harms, they also could be applied with the eugenics intention to provide greater "economic security and social comfort to a selected group of people," to use Huntington's terms, encouraging the best to have "larger families than certain other types" (1935: 22–23, 79). Selective measures could be applied not only to control North American and southern African Indigenous populations and within the U.S. via racist miscegenation and nonconsensual sterilizations, but also to help maintain and improve the self-determined supremacy of Euro-American citizens. Negative proposals to prevent damaging land use could be used to selectively undermine the continuance of "less suitable," that is, unethical Euro-American stock. And positive proposals

---

[84] Powell (2015) suggests the differences of slower reception and greater durability resulting from Leopold's thoughtful and poetic traits versus Vogt's and Osborn's more blunt deliveries (221–223).

encouraging beneficial land use could be used to privilege the continuance of their "more suitable [i.e., ethical] races or strains of blood," in Galton's terms, even if "indirectly."

For example, in "Erosion as a Menace" Leopold proposes government inspections for erosion control and to take away land titles from bad land owners (who were unwilling or unable to change) and give them to more "progressive," good ones within the "Nordic" population. With less specificity, in his 1947 "The Ecological Conscience," Leopold writes that "decent land-use should be accorded social rewards proportionate to its social importance," which is utmost. This would help activate "an internal change" at "the foundations of conduct" (Flader and Callicott, 1991: 338, 345). And, in his *Almanac*, Leopold recommends "social approbation for right actions: social disapproval for wrong actions," again, to help in the "operation" of an evolving land ethic. If the competence of land users had a heritable component and if environment shaped its expression, which, in turn, helped shape land, as Leopold thought, then conservation policies might be applied to improve land and to improve land ethical people, hand in hand, in a positive feedback loop countering the prevalent negative one.

As Huntington wrote, "no one can yet measure character exactly, and the precise contribution of either heredity or environment is problematical" (1935: 22–23). For the present, then, it was important to consider both essential in the evolution and/or development of a person or society. Nature and nurture proved hard to separate. In the twentieth century, on the heredity or "nature" end of a spectrum, questions about evolving populations involved geneticists. In a 1933 lecture delivered to scientists in the Southwest, Leopold had raised the question of whether the "mass-mind [i.e., the qualitatively average person] *wants to* extend its powers of comprehending the world in which it lives, or, granted the desire, *has the capacity to do so*" (Flader and Callicott, 1991: 192). The former question Leopold referred to the German-educated Spanish philosopher José Ortega y Gasset, the latter to geneticists, albeit working "with trepidations," he acknowledged (192; Warren, 2016: 248–252).

In a 1935 lecture titled "Land Pathology," Leopold again noted variations among U.S. conservationists, those with a merely utilitarian view of land, whose foci arose from "individual limitations," and those with fewer limitations who appreciated both beauty and utility of land (Flader and Callicott, 1991: 213). This was a "cleavage" that carried through into his *Almanac* in which those who regarded land "as a biota" and/or as "the collective organism" were also experiencing "the stirrings of an ecological conscience" (1949: 221, 223). In Darwinian evolution, individual variations and deviations that were heritable and enhanced an organism's competitiveness and thus survival would win out and be passed on to future generations, sustaining the population within its shifting ecological environment. Leopold, in an early use of the term "land-ethic" (see Warren, 2016: 149), in 1935, tied variations in human ethical capacities, such as the capacity to comprehend land more or less complexly, directly to intentional, eugenical selection. Although, he acknowledged, the science was still in early stages. The "breeding of ethics is as yet beyond our powers," Leopold wrote. "All science can do is safeguard the environment in which ethical mutations might take place," he said, matter-of-factly (Flader and Callicott, 1991: 215).[85] In his 1941 lecture, "Ecology and Politics," Leopold added that "individuals deviating from 'normal'" might serves as an "evolutionary 'safety device'" determining "our continuity" (Flader and Callicott, 1991: 286). This might be a silver lining in cases such as the overpopulation of Europe, he suggested. Presumably, the more Europeans the greater chance helpful deviations of heritable "cultural values" would emerge (284).

After World War II, scientists tried to separate themselves from associations with Nazi Germany's genocidal eugenics. At the same time, the role of environment in determining human behavior and society, which European natural historians and human geographers from the eighteenth century had promoted (Smith, 2021), became more prevalent. "Environment" would carry forward terms and schemes of scientific racism and, evidently, eugenics in yet new attire. As early as a 1925 article "Wilderness as a Form of Land Use," Leopold had linked the "pioneer environment" of early Euro-settlers over the past "three centuries with "the character of our racial stocks" determining "the character of our development" – "the very stuff America is made of" (Flader and Callicott, 1991: 137). Leopold thus had been concerned that the end of the frontier meant the end of the wilderness meant the end of Americans. Referring to the recurring self-exterminating potato bug story while approving of a proposal of the Russian philosopher P.D. Ouspensky, Leopold was explicit about the opposite possibility: that "the determining characteristic of rational beings is that their evolution is self-directed," individually and collectively (Flader and Callicott, 1991: 137, 142). By 1947, in "The Ecological Conscience," Leopold was still proposing self-directed evolution yet with "no illusions" about how fast a land ethical society could "become functional" contra Galton's belief in the best "strains," given the chance, "prevailing speedily." Leopold, nonetheless, was

---

[85] For philsophical underpinings of "a land ethic" or "the possible ethic," as Leopold also wrote, he acknowledged "Biological Ethics" (1932) by the Italian mammalogist Oscar De Beaux."Biological Ethics" featured a principle that to destroy what is not yours, that you did not make and cannot recreate, is to transgress a fundamental norm of biological ethics (Pedrotti, 2001: 40). This also hearkens to some of Hornaday's language, against extinction, which Leopold had echoed earlier in his career: "Man, with all his wisdom, has not evolved so much as a ground squirrel, a sparrow, or a clam." (And yet!) (Warren, 2016: 94).

clear about where society should head – *"throw your weight around* on matters of right and wrong in land use," he said (345–6). This would be to preserve the environment that made and would not only sustain, but could keep improving people.

The role of environment also tended to the "nurture" side of the spectrum, including attention to relations of heredity and social systems and the importance of outdoor recreation and education (Turda, 2012: 73). Leopold's grand narrative of ecological-evolutionary progress toward a land ethic put the biological and hereditary component of a human conscience into relationship with ecological land management, or land doctoring. In a sense, then, Leopold analogized not only in terms of animal populations but in terms of the larger purview of his scientific endeavor to tune capacities of animals to capacities of land. In *Game Management* Leopold proposed "the love of sport," hunting in particular, for those who possessed it, as capable of expanding into/with a conviction. The outdoorsman, that is, might come to understand that the human capacity to use land well rather than a high population density – which deteriorated the quality of both land and its human members – was the "true test" of whether "the average citizen" was "civilized," Leopold proposed. The "practice of game management" and the development of a "culture which will meet this test," accordingly, were the same thing (392, 423).

Furthermore, the desire to hunt, Leopold believed, involved an "instinct" for "combat" linked with "the biological basis of human nature" (391).[86] Thanks to what he regarded as the more recent inventions of agriculture and commerce for food supply, subsistence hunting – viewed as merely driven by hunger – could be superseded by a higher form. Sport hunting, that is, could be more advanced in "cultural value" (1949: 181) by virtue of adding an ethical component of self-limitation. That is, the hunter did not (need to) kill everything he could. In fact, the fewer mechanized gadgets the better for ethical development, Leopold suggested (1933: 391–392; 1949: 166, 178–180). That the inborn "ethical code" varied from hunter to hunter, according to Leopold, signaled that the advancement was still in progress thus offering a potential point of management intervention (391–392). Self-limitation, in those already predisposed, that is, might be expanded – via "recreational engineering" meaning "the development of the perceptive faculty in Americans" (1949: 173, 174) – to express a similar conviction regarding the greater ecological capacity of land. From Daniel-Booneing to hunting and

---

[86] Formerly, without dipping beneath the surface of geniality, I blithely titled an entire chapter of *Aldo Leopold's Odyssey* "The Germ and the Juggernaut," referencing Leopold's belief that "within human nature" lay "at least the 'germ of a better order of things'" (Warren 2016: 246, 253, 264). And, in *Odyssey*'s chapter "Wildlife and the New Man," I ignored the import of many signals, including "racial inheritance."

wilderness travel to the higher level, non-consumptive activities of nature study, wildlife research, and husbandry (173, 175, 185), supporting land health, including all degrees and sizes of wilderness, would further support the mutual improvement of wildlife and recreationalists, as Leopold continued to reckon in his *Almanac*. "In my opinion," Leopold wrote, "the promotion of wildlife research sports is the most important job confronting the profession of wildlife management." Promoting ecology as outdoor recreation would encourage the "search in animal populations for analogies to our own [population] problems." This was important to solving the vexing contradiction. It was "important to the whole human enterprise," Leopold continued to emphasize (186–187).[87]

As a faculty member at the University of Wisconsin, Leopold, in terms similar to those in *Game Management*, proposed, in a 1939 letter, that conservation education should "not stop at teaching techniques of biology and land use." It should, likewise, "bridge the gap between land use and human culture" (Warren, 2016: 269). That bridge he believed to be land ethical thinking and behavior. In a 1937 "Science Inquiry" publication, Leopold, who had chaired the report committee, reiterated that such an ethic was tied to a variable hereditary element within his target population, which were mostly Euro-American white, male students.[88] "Interest in wildlife is a racial inheritance. It does not persist in all individuals," the report said. "Where it does persist," it continued, "its cultivation and development are generally believed to be conducive to the 'good life'" (Leopold et al., 1937: 26; Warren, 2016: 272). Below the surface of such thoughtful, well-meaning ideas was the suggestion of selecting and nurturing future ecological-ethical land managers in evolutionary and eugenics senses. The next year Leopold took charge of drafting a statement of qualifications for "The Wildlife Society," newly minted, a sign of his expanding profession. This draft proposed to define a wildlife student in terms of "What He Is" alongside other criteria. Choice candidates cum graduates, for example, "should have" a "reasonably sound physique" and be "cooperative"; have a "better-than-average

---

[87] In negative terms, in 1946, Leopold was still listing "medicine" as.a factor contributing to the social strife accompanying human overpopulation analagous to "an overpopulated muskrat marsh" (Callicott and Freyfogle, 1999: 225). Left undiscovered by predators, Leopold explained in his 1941 lecture, the animals do the killing job themselves (Flader and Callicott, 1991: 283). Limiting reproduction voluntarily, though an option, "demands [unlikely] unanimity for its success" and might itself result in "decay of moral fiber," Leopold worried (284). Unanimity in a voluntary program, in particular, if intending, eugenically, to encourage bigger families among those deemed best and small or no children among the worst genetic stock.

[88] One woman, white and from a wealthy family, Frances Hamerstrom, graduated from Leopold's program. Her husband Frederick was the only person to earn a doctorate from the program. The couple served as research fellows under Leopold in 1940 (Wisconsin Conservation Hall of Fame. "Frederick and Frances Hamerstrom, https://wchf.org/frederick-and-frances-hamerstrom/; Temple, S. (2020). "Fran Hamerstrom." In USFS. *Women in Conservation*, www.fws.gov/sites/default/files/documents/2020-Conservation-History-journal.pdf.)

scholastic record"; already display "habitual self-teaching" (particularly in natural history); and, most importantly to Leopold, have the sort of "mind," which "defies" the "best efforts of all committees" to define and was "the aim of all education, including wildlife" (Warren, 2016: 277–278).[89]

In the *Almanac,* Leopold would urge that the "*content*" of conservation education define "right or wrong" in land use, assign "obligation," call for "sacrifice," and advance "change in the current philosophy of values" (1949: 207–208). He tied obligations to conscience and to the need to extend "social conscience from people to land." This extension called for an "internal change" reaching to the "foundations of conduct," the foundations from which spring "philosophy and religion" (209–210). The "evolution of a land ethic," Leopold stressed, "is an intellectual as well as emotional process" (225). It was an "affair of the mind as well as the heart," as he had written in "The Ecological Conscience," that "implies a capacity to study and learn, as well as to emote about the problems of conservation" (Callicott and Flader, 1991: 343). And that subject matter and those problems were complex. Leopold knew of "at least one certainty: the trend of evolution is to elaborate and diversify the biota" (1949: 216). Meanwhile, he explained, with increased "population density" and "the efficiency of tools," "modes of cooperation" for his powerful society had also become more complex (1949: 202). It was "a truism," Leopold wrote in his *Almanac,* "that as the ethical frontier advances from the individual to the community, its intellectual content increases" (225). This "affair" would take affection for and access to land, yes, but also an expansive and expanding "thinking" capacity (225) – a capacity that might be educated as well as inherited and thus managed – to use land skillfully and also to "release the evolutionary process for an ethic" (224).[90]

Expanding alongside this educational-evolutionary need, too, was the "development of the sciences," in the terms of Herbert Spencer. To Spencer's "natural sequence – from physics to sociology – Leopold added ecology as "the last science," that is, the most complex one. Ecology, "the sociology of the biota," was to be "predictive" and contribute to "social wisdom" (e.g., Flader and Callicott, 1991: 305; Callicott and Freyfogle: 1999, 219–220; Warren 2016: 271). Ecology was related at a "right angle" to biological evolution (Warren, 2016: 12), useful as something like "the frog in a railroad switch," which ends

---

[89] Leopold, A. (With Subcommittee). "Professional Training in Wildlife Management," 6 September draft, LP 9/25/10-2: 9(10): 1362–1371, 1364.

[90] LP 9/25/10-6 17(4): 900-01. To "release the evolutionary process for an ethic" was a matter of changing thinking, as a community. "Ontogeny repeats phylogeny," Leopold repeated twice in his *Almanac,* meaning "the development of each individual" – and, he said, the development of society – repeat the evolutionary history of the race" in "mental as well as physical things" (1949: 175–176, 178). When Leopold says he has "presented the land ethic as a product of social evolution," it would thus reach from philosophy to linkages with biological heredity.

up "routing the world's traffic,"⁹¹ Leopold's was a grand scheme, something like a new religion, or replacement for religion. He left behind, at his passing, plans for a new textbook on the field (Warren, 2016: 350). Ecology – with teeth – would help build "receptivity into the still unlovely human mind" by the arts of skilled land managers of "perception" (1949: 177). For this, it would take educating choice students as future ecological managers and educators.

For Leopold, as for others in his scientific circles, an educational challenge was purposefully "creating such men" who would be the "right people" for the job of teaching future generations, as Leopold put it in a January 5, 1948 correspondence with his close colleague, Roberts Mann.⁹² A land manager and fervent educator, Mann, in a letter dated December 16, 1947, had conveyed his concern to Leopold, quoting geneticist and demographer Robert C. Cook.⁹³ Conservation education, that is, might help prevent soil erosion by staving off "genetic erosion," in Cook's terms. "Soil is important, surely," he had written, "but what will it profit us to build a paradise for imbeciles." Cook, a contributor to Huntington's eugenics book, *Tomorrow's Children*, esteemed both nature and nurture in his thinking. He urged attention to human breeding, controlling human population, as well as teaching the "interrelationship of all things in nature, including man himself." Mixed with the biological and ecological were eugenicist and racist elements Mann had stressed in his letter, linking, also in his own words, "the education of our children" with the "future of our natural resources, and, therefore, of our human resources." Leopold, just months before his passing, had written to Mann: "I find myself completely in sympathy with what you say in your letter," which he would circulate "to our university committee on this very subject."⁹⁴ I find no record of Leopold eschewing

---

⁹¹ LP 9/25/10-6 17[4]: 900–901. In "The Role of Wildlife in a Liberal Education," Leopold explains his preference for "ecology as superior to evolution as a window from which to view the world," believing that "the mind of the average student" was not equipped to keep learning in that arena (Flader and Callicott, 1991: 305).

⁹² "I am inclined to agree with you that there will be employment for the right people," Leopold concluded to Mann: "I am circulating your letter to our university committee on this very subject" (LP 9/25/10-1: 2[8]: 674).

⁹³ Roberts Mann to Leopold, Letter, December 16, 1947, LP 9/25/10-1: 2[8]: 675–676. Known as an authority on population policy and eugenics, Cook was an advocate for birth control, particularly for parents deemed low in intelligence and class. He was known for raising the alarm over the ill effects of increasing human population. Cook worked at the Tucson Indian Training School, founded with the purpose of "assimilating children" after seizing them from Akimel Au-authm and Xalychidom Pipaash (Pima and Maricopa) and Tohono O'odham Tribes, ruthlessly forcing them to speak English and learn the customs of U.S. settler-colonial society (Barnes, B. (1991). "Demographer Robert Cook Dies," www.washingtonpost.com/archive/local/1991/01/09/demographer-robert-cook-dies-at-92/ddf0a5d9-5b9f-4557-b961-4922dc631ba9/; Library of Congress. "Robert C. Cook Papers: Collection Summary," https://findingaids.loc.gov/exist_collections/ead3pdf/mss/2011/ms011012.pdf).

⁹⁴ LP 9/25/10-1: 2(8): 675–676, 674. In a letter to his friend Morris Cooke in 1940, Leopold cautioned against thinking that "the 'total job' [of conservation] can be done without rebuilding

the troubling elements within the correspondence, which, albeit in his own more cautious ways, he himself had promoted. Even were there evidence of Leopold coming to resist eugenics and all forms of scientific oppression, as he had other harmful aspects of his culture and, even if he had lived long enough to do so, settler-colonialist power structures remain integrated into his writings and thus into any ongoing conservation legacies that do not question them.

Taken together, Leopold's vexing contradiction took up with a eugenics framework within a racist system. Within its own self-determined supreme culture, it sorts out those with better and worse genetic endowments and privileges, as most qualified, those already nurtured by colonial land-privilege (i.e., a "farm background" versus of "modern city life" in Mann's words (2); "rural betterment" in Huntington's terms (75); "pre-existing [outdoor] skill," "familiarity" with "farming" or "other land industries," and "natural history" experience in Leopold's [Warren, 2016: 277]).[95] This scheme casts shade on otherwise well-meaning recreational or scholarly education in caring, ecological understanding and in land health. It is to decide – with normalized, unjust arrangements intact – who continues to have access to land, and in what condition – who inherits it, for better or worse, and who doesn't.

Two years before Leopold's correspondence with Mann, *The Journal of Heredity* (an arm of the American Genetic Association), had republished a condensed version of an important essay by Leopold. "The Conservation Ethic," originally published in the *Journal of Forestry* in 1933, the year of *Game Management*'s publication. In 1946, the essay had been renamed "Racial Wisdom and Conservation." The editor of *The Journal of Heredity* was none other than Robert C. Cook. The introduction was addressed to "We people of the United States," a white readership. The framing stressed ecological interrelationship and credited Leopold's work as presenting "a scheme of concepts and relationships which could form ... [the] background" of "any awakening of a popular interest in eugenics." That is, it could help motivate "an attitude akin to the religious" or "a new faith," which Sir Francis Galton himself had called for, aimed at "the conservation of our race" (1946: 275).[96] By the 1940s,

---

Homo sapiens, or, to put it conversely, by government initiative alone" (Warren, 2016: 420 fn114).

[95] Leopold, A. (With Subcommittee). "Professional Training in Wildlife Management," 6 September draft, LP 9/25/10-2: 9(10): 1362–1371, 1364.

[96] In both editions of *Aldo Leopold's Odyssey*, I mentioned "Racial Wisdom and Conservation" in an awkward footnote in/with a move to innocence (416–417 fn37). A copy of "Racial Wisdom and Conservation" is located in Leopold's bound reprints with his library stamp. Imputing my own discomfort, I stressed uncertainty regarding Leopold's consent (whereas, I had not done so concerning other republished papers). I have not been alone in my hedging. Lin (2020 and quoted in Meine, 2022 fn11) claims: "There is no evidence that Leopold was aware of or acceded to this use of his article." Given the reprint's stamped presence in Leopold's library, it seems unlikely

Leopold had become increasingly aware of the complexity of land relations and far less sanguine about figuring out and manipulating "which levers to pull" to control them (Warren 2016: 130, 182). He knew that, faced with "so many conflicting needs," he did not have "a completely logical [conservation] philosophy all thought out" (Warren 264). At the same time, he was becoming more convinced of the need for "internal change" or "an ecological conscience" (Flader and Callicott, 1991: 338) and more pessimistic about whether and how long it would take to evolve (345, Warren, 2016: 255). Nor did he give up on sweeping narratives, which are prone to become totalizing, even fascistic.[97] While Leopold remained uncertain on whether and how geneticists

---

that he did not know of it, even if post-publication. I find no record of his objection to this publication. Given his later correspondence with Mann referencing Cook's work and the eugenics elements in Leopold's own work, he might even have been proud of it. Yet, without direct evidence, Leopold's awareness of, consent to, and opinions about "Racial Wisdom and Conservation" remain unproven. "The Conservation Ethic" first appeared in *The Journal of Forestry* in 1933. According to Flader and Callicott (1991: 358), it also was reprinted in the newsletter of Pan American Section of the International Committee for Bird Preservation and reprinted in part as "La ética de la conservación," *Boletín del departamento de conservación de Suelos,* Vol 1, in July 1948, a Venezuelan venue, as well as portions reprinted in the *Almanac,* and, again, in whole, as the 1933 version, in Flader and Callicott (1991: 181–192).

[97] There has been ongoing discussion among some environmental philosophers on whether Leopold's land ethic is fascistic and how or how not. (In the process of defending Leopold, for example, Nelson, 1996 surveys literature up to that date. Subsequent to that publication, Starkey, 2007 and Millstein, 2015, 2018 take up their own defenses and Salwén, 2014 pushes back, in the process, also surveying.) Arguments tend to center on the particular sense of fascism as calling for the sacrifice of individuals to the whole. This passage of Leopold's is often called upon: "A thing is right when it tends to preserve the integrity, stability, and beauty of the biotic community. It is wrong when it tends otherwise" (Leopold, 1949: 224). Although I am not a philosopher, I tend to agree with Millstein (2015) in not reading Leopold's *intent* as necessarily fascist, particularly when narrowed to this summary expression. Millstein argues that Leopold's ethic "implies respect for *fellow members* of the biotic community as well as respect for the community as such" (312). In fact, the sentence before Leopold's oft-cited lines allows for "economic expediency," which keys to self-interest, alongside what is "ethically and esthetically right" in guiding land use. Yet Leopold repeatedly enacts the violence of writing out Indigenous, as well as Black, and other non-white people. So a question worth emphasizing is: to whom might ecofascism in Leopold's concepts be or not be legible, and why? In this section, I read Leopold's *intent* as addressing the vexing contradiction, in yet another phrasing – that "our tools are better than we are, and grow better faster than we do" (Flader and Callicott, 1991: 254). Leopold's meaning of "we" is a white supremacist settler colonial one. And his response to the contradiction – his model of change, as it develops, en route to an "ecological conscience" – at worst, promotes and at best does not disavow racist, Malthusian, and eugenicist ideas. (In the *Almanac,* Leopold ties the often central quote just mentioned – on right and wrong in land use – to "a minority" exhibiting better/more complex thinking, tied to human nature as well as nurture, upon which the release of the evolution of an ethic depends [224]. This is followed by a recommendation for social practices to govern such evolution [225]. On the surface such governance and surely the encouragement of nature study seem reasonable and even desirable. Yet, looking deeper, a eugenics scheme floats below the surface). *In effect*, then, to the best of my lights, Leopold's ardent concern, while intending to eschew violence to land, justifies it toward particular people (e.g., 1949: 220) while upholding "exisiting systems of power and inequality," which is an historically informed definition of ecofascism (Anson, et al. [2022]. "Against the

and demographers and other social scientists would work out how to shorten evolutionary time to generate a functional land ethic, he did not disavow the possibility of eugenics. Waiting, he kept it at hand to mesh with potential remedies for the present moment.

Some rote portions of Leopold's 1933/1946 essay, others with minor changes, and key themes would remain integral to "The Land Ethic" and other parts of his *Almanac*.[98] The historical, ethical sequence, beginning with Odysseus, sets up all versions of the essay, which is a response, post-frontier – to the failures of various conservation-minded measures to guide or control private land users to protect public interests in land. The essay grapples with the realities of the evolutionary, co-determinations of conditions of humans, societies and environments, but not enslavement and colonization of Africans; with "dark and bloody ground," Boone, and the agency of Europeans and bluegrass, but not "the Native Indians;" with human "density" and Earth's "saturation," but not land theft and economic marginalization; with limits of "mass-mind" and intentions to nurture and bequeath, biologically, greater capacity; with science's importance, stressing ecology, remedial, predictive, and applied – so often to "step beyond 'science' in the narrow sense" (Freyfogle and Callicott, 1999: 226) – for bettering "society" yet still incorporating images and animal analogies threaded with bias into solving land-use problems while leaving unquestioned *Homo sapiens's* kingship or "dominion" – whether "self-perpetuating" or "self-destructive" – leaving intact assumptions of heteropatriarchal white supremacy. The essay versions articulate, as does the final paragraph of Leopold's *Almanac,* the vexing contradiction: "We are remodeling the Alhambra with a steam shovel" (1946: 278; 1949: 226).

Facing the vexing contradiction, there, in Leopold's unbridged "gap between land use and human culture," were and are entire Indigenous Nations, Black and

---

Ecofascist Creep," www.asle.org/wp-content/uploads/Against-the-Ecofascist-Creep.pdf; on "appeals to nature to justify violence" at the roots of U.S. "land logics" with the already large body of race and nature literature see Anson, A. [2023]. "No One Is a Virus," https://envhistnow.com/2023/09/06/no-one-is-a-virus-on-american-ecofascism/).

[98] Ellipses of two sentences to several paragraphs within the 1946 text indicate portions of the 1933 text not included. Most of the published text was unrevised, but there was some further condensing, and a few word changes. For instance, the exchange of "ecological" for "biological" in the "ethical sequence" of the *Almanac*. In 1933, "Christianity tries to integrate the individual to society, Democracy to integrate social organization to the individual" (Flader & Callicott, 1991: 182).) In 1946, "Christianity," rather than "Democracy," tries to integrate social organization to the individual (276); the reverse is not mentioned. In "The Land Ethic" (1949: 203), "Golden Rule" substitutes for "Christianity" in its 1933 role, and the sentence about "democracy" reoccurs. Also, "much less of justice" appears in 1933 (Flader & Callicott, 1991: 181) and 1946 (276), but not in the *Almanac* (1949: 201). Explicit reference to "geneticists" in 1933 and 1946 does not repeat in "The Land Ethic." Given other evidence, including subsequent writings and letters, I tend to think this was rhetorical and/or indicative of the scientific trend to distance from Nazism and/or of the science not being advanced enough for its desired applications, rather than indicative of a change of heart. For essays on making the *Almanac*: Callicott, 1987.

more racialized non-white, disabled, women, and otherwise suppressed people. It is difficult to imagine stable coalitions based on such erroneous conceptions of commonality between many North American Indigenous and Leopoldian "practical models for ethics," in Whyte's terms. "Many Indigenous ethics and knowledge systems have critical feedback loops built into them" and, like the Anishinaabe Water Walk, connect with on-the-ground "social justice transformations" and "anti-colonial action," he notes (2024). Whereas, a Leopoldian model of ethical change privileges the "best" Euro-Americans and menaces others *as if* doing so is disconnected from menacing land. Leopold's colonialist, conservationist model suppresses Indigenous presence – relegating and assimilating persons while taking homelands, and, as we shall see, surreptitiously appropriating shards of knowledge. Moreover, it turns out there is at least one prerequisite for participation in Leopold's "thinking community" in which a land ethic may evolve – that is, members must have minds with the capacity to think (225). Leopold's model of change assumes that this capacity inheres within Euro-Americans, albeit to greater and lesser degrees, but not, likewise, within Indigenous persons and other animals and beings who appear to him, if they appear at all, to lack intentional ethics, scientific knowledge systems, and/or innovative technologies. There may remain much to avow in Leopoldian narratives, including affection for land, challenging mere utilitarianism and "resource" extraction, and the humility of uncertainty that envisions people, open to change, thinking together. In the murkier underneath, however, Leopold's model recommends unethical extremes to bring about ethical improvement – from withholding medicine from other people's children to ranking the fitness of his own society's offspring and differentially privileging them. It calls for inhumanities in order to keep the ground underneath an Empire's dominion rather than to achieve justice in earth inheritance.

3.3 Epistemological Privilege: It Is Absurd

Leopold as much as anyone understood that thoughts have consequences. Indeed, I would almost say it became a mantra. "A conservationist is one who is humbly aware that with each stroke he is writing his signature on the face of his land," Leopold wrote in the *Almanac* essay "Axe-in-Hand" (Leopold, 1949: 68). In "The Land Ethic," he put it directly: "As a land-user thinketh, so is he" (Leopold, 1949: 225).[99] "An ethic," he explained in that essay, "presupposes the existence of some mental image of land as a biotic mechanism." The popular "balance of nature" concept, Leopold suggested, was not an apt symbol because it conjured a too-simple and too-static weighing scale. A "truer picture" or

---

[99] And, "The landscape of any farm is the owner's portrait of himself" (Flader and Callicott, 1991: 263).

"image" of complex land, he proposed – in his 1939 essay "A Biotic View of Land" and in the center of "The Land Ethic"—was a "biotic pyramid." This biotic or "land pyramid" became a core, organizing, ecological image of land health to which the land ethic pointed. It would be "a common concept," Leopold hoped, motivating and coordinating the social and natural sciences as well as land users in common cause (Flader and Callicott, 1991: 273). "We can be ethical," Leopold asserted, "only in relation to something we can see, feel, understand, love, or otherwise have faith in" (Leopold, 1949: 214). It follows, then, that *not* seeing, feeling, understanding, loving, or otherwise having faith in someone – whether Boricuas, southern Africans, African Americans, Latinas/os, Chinese, and/or distinct North American Indigenous Peoples – as they represent themselves – is itself an elimination with violent consequences. By the racist-colonialist crafting of wilderness conceptually, politically and physically, Leopold undercuts the ethical value of his "perfect norm" for land health. Removing and/or devaluing the presences of time immemorial land citizens from his mental image of land also undermines its ecological validity and that of scientific work that does not question this – an epistemic problem.

In the section of "The Land Ethic" detailing "The Land Pyramid" Leopold explained in the *Almanac* that "soil-oak-deer-Indian is a chain that has now been largely converted to soil-corn-cow-farmer" (Leopold, 1949: 215). As discussed also in the previous section, humans, variously, were integral to Leopold's ethical land health vision. Leopold studied and defended interrelations of soils, oaks, and deer integrated, he hoped, with "a new kind of farmer" (Warren, 2016: 420 fn114). As we are seeing from various angles, he did not, likewise, show faith in Native people, as valued and "thinking" human members of long "lines of dependency" (Leopold, 1949: 215), including many hunters and many farmers of more regenerative and/or productive methods and technologies compared with many Euro-American ones (Dunn, 1994; Mt. Pleasant, 2011).[100] The conversion of one chain into another explicitly assumes the elimination of Indigenous Peoples and does so without addressing injustice and respectful regard for the rippling consequences. Taking Leopold's norm as the ethical and practical standard for coalition-making is inapt. How could anyone expect Indigenous persons to express and legitimate, in Whyte's terms, "their systems of knowledge production" (2024) through a perspective that eliminates them and/or their thinking and is also therefore epistemologically troubled, for example, in gathering thus biased, unreliable observations? Any such expectation "can grant unsubstantiated and even offensive privilege,"

---

[100] Unless viewed as in the past, as ancient ones taking on a mythic quality that does not threaten the present.

in Whyte's terms, "in relation to Indigenous ethics." Doing so, indeed, "will have already suppressed them before dialogue has even begun" (Whyte, 2024). Where would be any chance for reciprocity, procedural justice, or stable coalitions when, for Indigenous people, "a common concept" of land means ongoing oppression besides untrustworthy "truth"?

Against their powerful resistance, the Apache Tribes were violently removed to military reservations by U.S. government agents, including from Leopold's forestry district – that is, from their ecologies, in which they would have been, in Leopold's terms, a "link in many chains" of dependency. Those government boundaries had also restrictively appropriated the areas of Buffalo hunts when there were still Buffalos.[101] Regardless of Apache compliance, in 1864, their citizens had been slaughtered by U.S. federal troops to make way for statehoods of the southwestern territories in which Leopold's career had begun. Though ruthlessly reduced in number by Euro-settlers, Apache and Buffalo lived and live on in resurgence.[102] Leopold had not named Apache in his 1923 essay as one of the "races" or "cultures" leaving "the earth alive, undamaged" (Flader and Callicott, 1991: 96). Merely implicitly, and shudderingly, he does so in his 1937 essay "Conservationist in Mexico." Here, Leopold begins by attributing healthier land in "Chihuahua" to settlers' fears of Apache, which, ironically, protected land from themselves. "The predatory Apache of our Southwest," Leopold wrote, "was early rounded up and confined in reservations, whereas

---

[101] "The impact of civilization destroys many species of wildlife, some unavoidably (buffalo), many without real reason (woods wildflowers)," Leopold wrote in a 1941 draft, "Planning for Wildlife" (Callicott and Freyfogle, 1999: 194). "No one debates the removal of the buffalo or the pigeon from the cornbelt," he wrote in a 1946 draft, "The Land-Health Concept and Conservation" (221). In the *Almanac*, Leopold wrote that "the culture of primitive peoples is often based on wildlife." His example was the dependencies of the "plains Indians" (this would include the Apache Tribe of Oklahoma)on buffalo (1949: 177). For the buffalo, the Tribes, and the connection between them, this is beyond pragmatic; it is callous, unspeakably so. Also in the *Almanac* is his elegy for Passenger Pigeons, which praised the "new knowledge" of Darwinian science indicating "that men are only fellow-voyagers with other creatures in the odyssey of evolution," which "should have given us, by this time, a sense of kinship with fellow-creatures," with attendant ethics (1949: 108–112). Altogether, again, he tends environmental fracture, in Ferdinand's terms, again, and maintains if not widens the colonial (i.e., also racist) one.

[102] For instance, regarding collective continuance and resurgency, the Mescalero Apache Tribe (Lipan and Chiricahua): "Our Apache elderly people are highly respected." Examples of how to properly approach elders are "practiced by the younger generation and the middle aged today on the reservation." The Tribe's "Cattle Growers" produce "high-quality commercial beef cattle while helping to conserve the natural resources of the tribe," a new "tradition" ("Welcome to Our Sacred Lands," https://mescaleroapachetribe.com). The Texas Tribal Buffalo Project is reconecting Lipan Apache and other Indigenous relatives to each other and (Buffalo) as relatives,.practicing "regenerative agriculture and Traditional Ecological Knowledge Skills" ("About Us," www.texastribalbuffaloproject.org/ttbp-mission-vision). Jicarilla Apache manage their Reservation's Game and Fish Department, with a "world-class big-game hunting program" (Jicarilla Apache Game and Fish, "Premier Destination," www.jicarillahunt.com/pages/about).

across the line in Mexico he was, until his recent near-extinction, allowed to run at large. Therefore our southwestern mountains are now badly gutted by erosion, whereas the Sierra Madre range across the line still retains the virgin stability of its soils and all the natural beauty that goes with the enviable condition" (Flader and Callicott, 1991: 239).

Here Leopold repeats a pattern. As also discussed in Section 3.1, he relegates Apache Tribes not only as inconvenient parts of wilderness, physically, but outside (superior) humanity, conceptually, and thus outside of intentional land-keeping ethics and intelligence as he did other wildlife, including carnivores. That is, when "allowed to run at large," "predatory" Apache prevented rapacious settlers (also without a land ethic, but with the capacity to evolve and intentionally innovate) from ruining the "virgin stability" of the Sierra Madre. As Mvskoke-Creek, Cheraw, Cherokee, Jewish, and Euro-American descendant, scholar and Native seed conservationist Noah Schlager argues, implicit in Leopold's observations, as a Yale-trained forest manager, is the view that "a forest without Indians is better than a forest with Indians, which is better than a barren mountainside." This valuation, present in the U.S. conservation movement from the start, Schlager stresses, and woven into Leopold's narratives, is a political legacy with very real on-the-ground, anti-Indigenous consequences.[103] It is also an epistemological legacy denying, assimilating, and/or appropriating credit for Indigenous knowledge production and sustainable land use while continuing to insist that Euro-Americans know and can do better.

Schlager finds a "most damning" remark of Leopold's in a 1909 letter to his brother *explicit content follows*: "The only hunting I've done this month," Leopold complained, "is for Indians. We caught a bunch in poaching and did some night-maneuvers – regular Daniel Boone style – but the s-of-bs got away from us. Old red and I chased them licked split plumb to the reservation line, but they foxed us for fair and got one of our horses to boot, Old Red buck I was going to buy him too, and sure hate to give him up."[104] This letter also verifies

---

[103] Noah Schlager (2018), "Unpacking F&ES's [at Yale] Colonial History," www.facebook.com/EnvironmentalJusticeAtYale/videos/unpacking-fess-colonial-history/112479829621117/.
And, I am proposing, it is a scientific legacy with very real consequences to the validity of research.

[104] Leopold. (November 11, 1909). Letter to Carl (brother), LP 9/25/10-8, 7(1):25. Five years earlier, at Lawrenceville, young Leopold sounded impressed by the outdoor curiosity and "unfathomable" words of "the novelty in the way of a lecturer," of Ohiyesa (Charles Eastman, Santee Dakota). Leopold presumed to know what "a true Indian" spoke like. He stressed his "fine build" and nature and spiritual wisdom, which only "those who have understanding" could hear, including himself, I suppose (Leopold. [February 10, 1904] Letter to Mother, LP 9/25/10-8, 4[2]: 111–121). Throughout Leopold's career, as we see throughout this Element, he participated in relegating, assimilating, and appropriating lands and knowledges from Indigenous Peoples. He viewed Indigenous Peoples as outcompeted by

that Leopold had understood Daniel Boone to be a hunter of "Indians" when he mentioned him in "The Conservation Ethic," "Racial Wisdom and Conservation," and, later, in "Wildlife in American Culture" and "The Land Ethic" in his *Almanac*.

A particularly telling instance of on-the-ground anti-Indigenous consequences of Leopold's anti-Indigenous political and epistemological relegations was his mid-1910s alignment with the unsuccessful U.S. effort to appropriate a 2,000-acre marsh within the Jicarilla-Apache Indian Reservation for a federal bird refuge. A "paradise," he called it, of "grassy shores ... blue mountain sky ... Just solid ducks" (Brown and Carmony, 1990: 25). The ethics and knowledge production of Jicarilla-Apache that aligned with this flourishing are not considered. Meanwhile, Hornaday-style, before they had parted ways on refuge management, Leopold had wanted to fence the marsh (to protect nests from wandering cows and sheep), prohibit hunting, and "clean out the varmints" that is, "predatory animals" (26, 27). Leopold hoped thus to double the "crop" of birds as a source that would overflow into other areas. "Nobody lives there," Leopold wrote, so "why not? ... It will benefit all and hurt nobody" (26). There were plenty of other shooting grounds, he said. By to "benefit all," he meant to benefit a public beyond a group of "twenty wealthy Colorado sportsmen" who wanted it as a shooting club (Brown and Carmony, 1990: 25–32; 27; Cryer, 2015). Leopold's "nobody lives there" was to imagine the very real intended removal of Jicarilla Apache, whom he knew were at home with that marsh, in order to support more settlers' enjoyment.

In a later settler fantasy set across that U.S.-Mexican border in homelands of Apache and more Tribes that were still "so lovely" and with "virgin stability" (Flader and Callicott, 1991: 239) – Leopold renders an almost poetic expression of Schlager's thesis as well as of "The Biotic Pyramid" food chain conversion. Leopold, in the *Almanac's* "Song of the Gavilan," imagines an old buck, a great oak, and the ancient masonry of an "old Indian"[105] – now ghostly – flooded by energy as a wilderness centerpiece – a symbolic structure

---

Euroamericans. Yet, in resonance with his belief in safe-keeping all the "parts" of land (e.g., "Engineering and Conservation," [Flader and Callicott, 1991: 253]; "Conservation," [Leopold, L. 1993: 147]), he could see it also was worth keeping remnants of Indigenous cultures (e.g., "the last little [Pueblo] fragment" [Flader and Callicott, 1991: 102]). In the *Almanac* Leopold allowed for "Indians," restrictively, as humans – as spiritual yet not intellectual animals and without agency to "control" nature (e.g., in "Odyssey"); as mysterious, passed on and ghostly (e.g., in "Song of the Gavilan"); and, disrespecting self-determination of Indigenous communities, he played at settler-Indigenous replacement (e.g., in "Song of the Gavilan").

[105] The Rio Gavilan watershed: Traditional lands of Indigenous Peoples – Paquime, Opata, and Apache – for at least a millennium. A Mestizo culture emerged after Spanish colonization and the Mexican nation-state (Fleming and Forbes, 2006; Taffa, D. [2023]. "Race and Class in New Mexico," https://searchlightnm.org/race-and-class-in-new-mexico/).

of a dynamic biotic pyramid. It is of course a symbol of Leopold's common concept of land, central to that of land health. Leopold saw the buck and himself as "actors in an [eternal] allegory" (Leopold: 1949, 151; Warren, 2016: 223–226). Underpinning the allegory, again, is the elimination of Indigenous inhabitants – their charming technologies appearing at the same time they are disappearing in the dim light of some mythical past – with settler bodies and ecologies as replacements.

A third example of anti-Indigenous appropriation along with assimilation is particularly knotty, explicitly involving Indigenous land and Indigenous scientific-ecological knowledge. In this case, Leopold discredits Indigenous expertise while later taking credit for it. Leopold's 1920 article, "'Piute [*sic*] Forestry' vs. Forest Fire Prevention," was an unusually sloppy piece of work, full of both uncited and also ungrounded claims. The essay was laced with condescending inaccuracies regarding Paiute Peoples (see also Lefler, 2014). "It is, of course, absurd," Leopold wrote, "to assume that ['the California'] Indians fired the forests with any idea of forest conservation in mind" (Brown and Carmony, 1990: 141). Demeaning ethical-scientific knowledges of Paiute, Leopold alleged that all presumably Euro-settler "old-timers" knew that "the Indian" burned forests simply in order to get game to stand still. He followed this with still other affronts: "A bunch of deer with their heads in the air waiting for a fire," Leopold claimed, "presented an easy mark, *even* [italics mine] to the Indian's bow and arrow." It was, he continued, "this fact and not any desire for fancied forest conservation which caused the Indians to burn forests" (Brown and Carmony, 1990: 142). Alongside the slur on Paiute hunting skill and technology, this so-called fact Leopold asserted about fire was completely unfounded. Indeed, as Schlager points out, Paiute have a long oral history of intentional burns for fire management as well as for hunting (2018). Leopold concluded his article with an accusation that the "light burning" practiced by Paiute had "destructive effects." These included "valuable forests ... gradually reverted to brush," with destroyed reproductive potential. According to Leopold, it was prevention of forest fires by the USFS, for which he worked, that was now bringing back regeneration.

Four years later, Leopold revisited fire ecology in "Grass, Brush, Timber, and Fire in Southern Arizona" (Flader and Callicott, 1991:114–122). He corrected his earlier mistaken scientific assertions with quite brilliant analyses. He admitted that "lightning and Indians kept the brush thin" with fires before "settlement of the country." The method of light burning, Leopold explained, "gave grass the upper hand ... this grass prevented [soil] erosion (115–116). In other words, although the landscape was altered, it remained intact and fertile. It was the settlers – as Leopold characteristically critiqued his own culture's poor land-use – who caused the grass to be removed by "great herds of livestock" (116). Grass had prevented fire, while grazing released ungrazeable brush and set fertility downhill, with ground succeeding into revivals of fire-vulnerable piñon woodlands, moreover, likely reducing some game numbers.

Leopold concluded with a sleight of hand that retrieved any credit he might have attributed to the Paiute. He wrote that "the *virgin* condition previous to settlement" was not a "climax" condition of forest but "a temporary type due to some kind of *damage*" (italics mine) (116). With this stunning phrasing, Leopold disappeared the Paiute (at least as logical-ethical human beings), since "virgin" meant "uninhabited" (at least by "Christians" or racialized white people), and ready for taking, to many white settlers, including conservationists. At the same time, he implicitly blamed the Paiute for a "damaged" landscape. But this directly contradicts what he had just remarked, "grass prevented erosion." Leopold neither acknowledged nor tried to repair his past mistakes and offenses. Furthermore, he assimilated into his own work supposedly "new" knowledge appropriated from the Paiute, who for many generations had collaborated with forces of fire-plant-soil interrelations.

Left unquestioned, Leopold's claims perpetuate a swelling historical narrative of Euro-American moral and knowledge-based ascendancy rooted in an entitled pioneer "cultural inheritance" and ecological-evolutionary improvement of land and people via conservation. This appears, in Whyte's words, as "literally the exact reverse of what numerous contemporary Indigenous people would see as the evolution of their ethics" (2024). As detailed in the previous Section 3.2, faced with the vexing contradiction of self-determined Euro-American superiority side by side with land ruination, Leopold's model of change enmeshes with Malthusian and eugenic concepts and relations that are also racist. This is a model contrary to Indigenous ones "connected to social justice transformations," which Whyte discusses. As highlighted in this section, Leopold's ecological concept of complex land at once writes out and appropriates from Indigenous "systems of ethics and knowledge production," in Whyte's words, with very real on-the-ground anti-Indigenous consequences, in Schlager's terms. Erasing Indigenous people, their systems of knowledge production, and actions based on them undercuts settler sciences operating on such a model. It does so while continuing to procedurally suppress those Indigenous knowledge systems that, in Whyte's terms, "have critical feedback loops built into them" and to suppress "self-critical" contemporary Indigenous Peoples who "have their own ideas about how to integrate Western science with their traditions" (2024). Such issues, as Whyte says, "complicate any attempt to compare versions of Leopoldian and Indigenous ethics" and "must be reckoned with by any actual attempts to bring people together around the idea of a similar orientation to environmental ethics" (Whyte, 2015: 8, 11; 2024) on the way to possibly bringing about any genuine, stable coalitions – if not any "thinking community" (Leopold, 1949: 225) – of "people of all heritages" (Whyte, 2024).

4 Self-Critiquing Rote Repetition (A Redux)

Two-term U.S. Poet Laureate Natasha Trethewey summarizes some of my best intentions in this Element in her essay "On Whitman, Civil War Memory, and My South." "I'm not interested in arguing the omissions of the past," she writes, "only the restoration of those omissions in the present." "Perhaps not restoration: acknowledgment is a better word" (Trethewey, 2005: 56). In a good way, I need Trethewey's help in looking at my own work, at the Leopoldian legacy, and acknowledging the omissions I have perpetuated. This literary study has surfaced many past offenses and attempted to set them in the present in order not to repeat them in the future (see Morrison, 1992). Here, I draw out a narratively pivotal, personal example of how colonialist white supremacy keeps hidden, until, intentionally, it is not.

In the first chapter of *Aldo Leopold's Odyssey*, "Seed Plots," I told a story about "America's world poet," Walt Whitman, whom Leopold sometimes recalled (Warren, 2016: 229, 345). The scene was Whitman's first trip to the West, by train in 1879. He was headed to the new, 38th U.S. state of Colorado. Whitman, I wrote, "took in the colors and winds." Out the moving window of the train, he "observed the flora, fauna, and people, and wrote about what he called 'America's characteristic landscape.'" "Seed plots of American character," U.S. historian Frederick Jackson Turner called the forests-turned-gardens, with white pioneers founding colonial settlements and the settler population expanding east to west (29–30). In Turner's words, the typical settler displayed "faith in man, hope for democracy, belief in America's destiny" (21–22) that would be, in clearer terms, belief in manifest destiny. If Eastern forests were "seed plots of American character," I suggested in this opening chapter, the West's prairies and grasslands might have "fed the American spirit" (29).

What most impressed Whitman, the New Yorker, about the landscapes he was seeing for the first time was "that feature of the topography of your western central world – that vast Something, stretching out on its own unbounded scale, unconfined, which there is in these prairies, combining the real and the ideal, and beautiful as dreams.'" At the same time, Whitman was impressed by his perception of the "inexhaustible land" and the "capacity and sure future destiny of that plain and prairie area." Whitman celebrated this "land of ten million virgin farms – to the eye at present wild and unproductive – yet," he enthused, "experts say that upon it when irrigated may easily be grown enough wheat to feed the world" (29–30).

In response to the poet, I observed – shrewdly, I thought – that Whitman apparently had not perceived the "sleeping tension" between the heavy cropping of this "inexhaustible land" for "wheat to feed the world," and, even were it inexhaustible, the need to keep vibrant the spiritual and "esthetic sense ... [of] that vast Something." "Was it possible to have both – the farms *and* the intangible essences, nature's wild beauty *and* expanding wealth?" I wondered. "If the question earlier went unasked within Whitman's musings, Leopold would address it in earnest," I continued, launching a key thesis of *Aldo Leopold's Odyssey*. Leopold's idea of "land health," the centerpiece of his work and of mine, emerged from this "sleeping tension" (Warren, 2016: 30).

Yet, like Whitman and Leopold, I did not see a whole picture. My argument excluded a fuller history. Like Whitman and Leopold, as I peered out the moving train's windows, I had conceptually relegated, appropriated, and assimilated the Indigenous Nations, past, present, and future generations, ignored abducted and enslaved Africans, dispossessed Mexican American families and all generations of land relations and knowledges of all of these and many more marginalized peoples and the dominating assumptions, projects, and structures that keep oppressing. I had omitted from my view out the window any who did not conform with my supremacist norm for recognition. My omissions were rote, remained normalized and as invisible to me as I let them be. I could have done better.

Trethewey is both generous and acute in her reflections on Whitman. She discusses Whitman's "prediction that the real war would not get into the books" (2005: 54). He believed much of that real history was too unpleasant for settler Americans to stomach. She recounts Whitman's projection that generations later, "when the grave has quenched many hot prejudices and vitalities, and an entirely new class of thinkers and writers come to the argument, the complete question, can perhaps be fairly weighed" (56). Meanwhile, Whitman wrote racist rants as harsh as any (Dunbar-Ortiz, 2014: 117–118). Hostility slightly submerged, in his own war-time poem "Ethiopia Saluting the Colors," he adhered to settler-comforting historical myopia. As Trethewey notes, Whitman "focuses on a 'dusky woman, so ancient hardly human,' and not black soldiers who were participants in the war rather than bystanders" (56). We can find similar dismissals in other poems. In "Yonnondio," for example, "Amid the wilds," Whitman sees, "swarms of stalwart chieftains, medicine-men, and warriors, / As flitting by like clouds of ghosts." These spiritual, warring figures, "(Race of the woods)," appear to him, for just a moment, in relief against "the cities, farms, factories" before blanking out "utterly lost." They have no future, only a past.

In *Aldo Leopold's Odyssey* I perpetuated my cultural ancestors' imaginaries of vague, cloudy ghosts, disappearing memories, "nameless men by nameless rivers," better or worse "human stocks," conversions of "the [old] Indian" to (a hopefully forthcoming "new kind of") "farmer." The imaginaries were part of, and perpetuated by, the master historical story incorporating manifest destiny, white supremacy, genocide, and eugenics. These are based upon a "logic of elimination," in Wolfe's terms, that still menaces now-living Peoples and their children.[106] Like my cultural ancestors, Whitman and Leopold, I paid keen attention to losses of Silphium, wolves, and soils' fertility, and I celebrated colors, winds, and the "vast Something." The "vast Something," in all these visions, is directly connected to Lands, east to west, north to south that Whitman, Leopold, and I have envisioned as virgin or raw wilderness, as standards for productive, settler-inhabited land health, the dream of the land ethic. In solidarity with "deep narrative and ontological revision," in Tallbear's terms, I acknowledge that we Euro-settlers stole and still profit from living lands that remain customary geographies of sovereign Indigenous Peoples. In the process, through violence and witlessness, we have disrupted and obstructed Indigenous collective continuance with attendant, reciprocal kinship responsibilities and rights to struggle and innovate free of systemic tyranny. We have done so, also undermining conditions for our own necessarily interdependent thriving, while claiming ethical and intellectual superiority.

When Whitman arrived in Colorado, and when Leopold arrived in Arizona and New Mexico, it had been mere decades or less since this region, also explored and colonized by the Spanish, was then forcibly annexed from Mexico, the Treaty of Guadalupe Hidalgo broken, one of the many treaties broken by the U.S. What Leopold saw as previous races or cultures, Ancestral Puebloans until late thirteenth-century drought, and, generations of Arapaho, Cheyenne, Ute nations, diverse Puebloans, Navajo, Apache, and Paiute – these Indigenous Peoples are still here. Indigenous Peoples are still everywhere, worldwide. Mexican Americans also are still fighting, learning from/with/as "the peoples who embody survival and defiance." In the words of Chicana feminist writer-activist Enriqueta Vásquez, "If there is a whole truth, it must come from the people who have been able to endure for thousands of years'" (Ybarra, 2022: 33–34). Indigenous Peoples are not only still here, they are safekeeping a wide majority of lands' biodiversity to date tied with climate habitability (Sobrevilla, 2008; Davis and Todd, 2017; Sultana, 2022; Hernandez, 2022). It is their cultural inheritances, their ecologies, that the

---

[106] Leaving Indigenous peoples fuzzy ... As I did (Warren, 2011; Warren, 2006, 3: Not only "ancient" people, but still-present Suma, Conchos, and Eudeve, Apache and relations).

U.S. colonialist-empire unvirtuously and unskillfully occupies, ultimately, to everyone's hurt.

The ethical catastrophe not to see, not to love, is not a mistake, but my birth culture's intentional settler-colonialism, which is inseparable from heteropatriarchal white supremacy and also its ableism. When I do not follow the leads of my discomfort – for instance, in silently perpetuating the ancestral vision of an inevitable ascent of the "Anglo-Saxon character" in Whitman's terms – the wrong adheres also in me (quoted in Dunbar-Ortiz, 2014: 118). This racist reality in manifest, ruthless expressions was always integral, moreover, with the tension I felt between "wheat to feed the world" and the "Vast Something." It has always been integral to U.S. conservation. The troubles are enmeshed within even the most well-meaning Leopoldian schemes, including of wildlife refuges, wilderness, ethical evolution, the land health concept, recreational and education ventures, knowledge production, and thinking communities. In addition to avowing what can be avowed and refusing what must be refused in the ancestral, Leopoldian legacy, there are the possibilities of rejoindering past proposals toward stable coalition building between people privileged and/or dispossessed by settler colonialism. One possible alternative is for settlers to learn how to listen to those enduring frontlines oppression – by the system of our heritage – openly, without imposing our own agendas. This includes efforts to hear differences between Leopoldian and Indigenist ethics while unlearning our oppressor defensiveness, as Whyte proposes. Attuning incorporates *seeking to not* know (Robinson, 2020) and acknowledging that we may *not* be understanding "what all the issues may be" as much as we might want to think we do (Whyte, 2015: 15; 2024).

5 Settler Listening as Rejoinder: Alaska Native Storytelling

Upholding common concerns without continuing to repeat past offences requires settler-conservationists to listen for differences. This can help us face ancestors genuinely, in Robert Pogue Harrison's terms, and in becoming the kinds of ancestors we'd like to be. Openness to difference, that is, can help guide choices between ancestral retrievals, renewals, and refusals, also reciprocated with rejoinders. That openness can point the way to other possibilities. Intralegacy and intergenerational conversations might help stabilize intercultural coalitions and make good relations expressing unity (versus universality) and a plurality of liberated Earth communities (Tallbear, 2019; Kanngieser and Todd, 2020; Whyte, 2020). Conversations may be sparked by recognizing, receptively listening to, un/learning from, and consensually acknowledging and/or stepping back to unoccupy the possibilities of others' – particularly

Indigenous – heritages. This may be on the way to "something like the abolition" of "race/ism," to invalidating the "logic of elimination," to breaking the relentless "settler-native-slave triad" to decolonizing, to the "repatriation of Indigenous land and life," liberating "minds, bodies, and lands," and "overturning the colonial structure and realizing Indigenous liberation" (Wolfe, 2006; Tuck and Yang, 2012; Dotson, 2018; McLean, 2020).[107] This might help ground any possibilities for future re/generative conditions of land and human beings' inseparable survival if not flourishing.

With so much in mind, I bear witness, with consent of storytellers and having been an invited participant, to three public episodes, events led by Iñupiat and Yup'ik and Athabascan persons, particularly of Gwich'in, Ahtna, Diné (Navajo) also of Sugpiaq and Tohono O'odham Peoples. In these episodes, according to my intergenerational methodology, this listening to attune is a rejoinder to colonialist-white supremacist systematized habits of relegating, appropriating, and assimilating others in Leopoldian narratives incorporating bad history; various manifestations of scientific racism and eugenics determining intergenerational land access; and a norm of epistemological hubris, which I have refused in 3.1, 3.2, and 3.3. Corresponding with my method, my observations are organized by Whyte's three crucial issues of comparison between Leopoldian and many Indigenous North American ethics, witnessing: (1) Alaska Native historical narratives of ethical trajectories since colonization counter to Leopold's unsound ethical-historical narrative, (2) Alaska Native inheritances difficult to translate into any English-language concepts and relationships, including Leopoldian ones, and (3) enactments of epistemological self-determination, irrespective of Leopoldian scientific schemes. These episodes may excite more widely reorganized settler responsibilities to listen for multiple scales of values from starting points that may/no longer be called "wilderness," unsettling ourselves.

In each episode, I pay attention to incommensurabilities of languages and other cultural-translational challenges. It is worth repeating that even when any of us try our best to understand each other, there is always the chance that we can't. This anti-racist, ontological challenge to Leopoldian humility also might be part of Whyte's coming "together as people of all heritages when we face differences" (2024) so as not to continue privileging a (and any) dominating group or "interpretative frameworks." It is akin to Harrison's caution to potential non-consanguineous relations who need to, but can't always, understand ways-of-telling. Humility renewed and revisioned points, again, to the insights of Robin Kimmerer. Her storytelling leads away from the hoarding disposition

---

[107] www.nativemovement.org.

whom she knows from her Anishinaabeg legends as Windigo, and, at the same time, away from settler-colonialists presuming they can become "Indigenous" in their lifetimes. Kimmerer orients settlers, rather, towards the possibility to "become naturalized to place" as anyone would need to become a citizen of a foreign nation in a lifetime. In political terms, if one who is "foreign-born" would, to become a citizen, "pledge to uphold the laws of the [U.S.] state. They might well uphold Nanabozho's Original Instructions, too," she writes, referencing her (and Whyte's) Anishinaabe ways of life. To "strive to become naturalized to place," Kimmerer suggests, means to throw off the "mind-set of the immigrant." It would be a practice of give-and-take – reciprocities – as if your life and others' depended upon it – body, mind, and spirit – across generations. It also would be, she says, to "know that your ancestors lie in this ground ... to live as if your children's future matters" inseparable from land – not lost, and found (Kimmerer, 2013: 214–215).[108]

5.1 Indigenous Histories: Many Names, Many Languages

Leopold aimed to reverse his dominating culture's land-ruining assumptions by extending a historic narrative of progress to incorporate good land use. Pioneers spread and hammered out "America" from "raw wilderness," Leopold asserted. Now that "mechanization assured us of a good breakfast," watching television, and with "the whole world" being "so greedy for more bathtubs" (1949: vii–ix), he argued, survival relied on his assimilative notion of *Homo sapiens* evolving their first land ethic. This, he went on to project, was occurring stepwise, with moral regard expanding from relations of man-to-man and man-to-society to man-society-land-community relations. The ethically expanded community would further appropriate "tag-ends" of wilderness, in other words, customary geographies of Indigenous Peoples – that is, of citizens of self-governing, politically distinct, land-based peoplehoods pre-existing any invasion or colonization (Kimmerer, 2013: 214–215; Whyte 2014: 144; Kolopenuk, 2020: S24) – who were to be relegated by assimilation and death (with the exception of a few protected few tag-ends of themselves). These stolen, relationally disrupted ecologies were to be taken as the "most perfect norm" by which to gauge improvements in land use. For Leopold, Alaska was a "blank place," albeit a valuable one. It was a vast, "virgin country," casting, in Robert Service's words, "the spell of the Yukon" on visitors. And many

---

[108] How do members of a colonizing culture challenge the systemic and habitual "resilience of settler privilege" (Whyte, 2018b) upon/if finding a dearth of potential "reciprocative rejoinders" (Harrison, 102–103) among our own legacies? How not to offend and repeat extractive tendencies when recognizing, finally, our (anti-Romantic) need for the help of Indigenous Peoples' land-flourishing knowledge and skills? Any such recognition would include valuing and supporting, for example, Indigenous "consent, diplomacy, trust, and redundancy" (Whyte, 2018a, Whyte et al., 2018).

of those visitors, even today, may think the poet captured the spell in his account of lone, "nameless men," "nameless rivers," and "strange valleys" (Leopold, 1949: 176, 191; Service, 1909; see also Smith, 2021).[109]

In summer 2019, along the banks of the Yukon River, I gathered with Indigenous people – many whose names I already knew from living in traditional territories of the lower Tanana Dene Peoples and the Dena'ina Peoples occupied by Fairbanks, Alaska. Here, generations of Indigenous Peoples have lived for millennia, from time immemorial, on still-unceded lands, and they are still here, distinct from the U.S. and Canadian empires surrounding them. That June, I attended the first Arctic Indigenous Climate Summit organized by the Gwich'in Steering Committee directed by Bernadette Demientieff (Gwich'in Steering Committee, 2020). It was hosted by her village of Gwich'yaa Zhee (Fort Yukon, Alaska), one of some fifteen communities of the Gwich'in Nation, spread along the vast arctic migration route of vadzaih (the Porcupine Caribou Herd), which crosses the current U.S.-Canada border. "We [Gwich'in] believe that we each have a piece of caribou in our heart and the caribou have a piece of us in their heart," Demientieff has said.[110] There was "a vow," she explains, "that we would always take care of each other" (16).

On the third day of the gathering, Enei Begaye, executive director of Native Movement, called participants together under an Octagon canopy. She invited us there to share in an activity created by Yup'ik elders of the Mamterilleq (Bethel) region. Begaye noted that she did so with the consent of Rose Domnick, whom she knew as one such elder and community leader, who had taught it to her. With Begaye's consent, I pass on this abbreviated depiction. The activity had much more to it than can be shared here.[111]

Begaye placed a drum on the ground. This drum represents the core, she explained, beginning an ethical narrative that runs directly counter to the Leopoldian one. This core is everything that connects to Mother Earth. It centers many Indigenous worldviews, she said.

Begaye is Diné (Navajo) and Tohono O'odham, a mother with a Neets'aii Gwich'in partner. Earlier, Begaye also had retold a story passed on from some of her grandparents. They recalled them saying that when Dene/Athabascan

---

[109] Service, R. (1909). *Ballads of a Cheechako*, https://www.gutenberg.org/files/259/259-h/259-h.htm, #2; and (1954); "The Spell of the Yukon" at https://www.poetryfoundation.org/poems/46643/the-spell-of-the-yukon.

[110] Demientieff, B. (2019). "Statement of Bernadette Demientieff, Executive Director, Gwich'in Steering Committee to the U.S. House of Representatives Committee on Natural Resources, Subcommittee on Energy and Mineral Resources hearing "The Need to Protect the Arctic National Refuge Coastal Plain" on H.R. 1146, The Arctic Cultural and Coastal Plain Protection Act," https://www.congress.gov/116/meeting/house/109126/witnesses/HHRG-116-II06-Wstate-DemientieffB-20190326.pdf. Many sources can be located at https://defendingthearcticrefuge.com.

[111] Personal email, 12/11/2020. Thank you, again, Enei.

Peoples of the north and south meet – maybe as in their partnership, and as in what is happening here at the Summit – it would mean the end of the world.[112] This would mean, they clarified, that so much change had occurred that the formerly recognizable world was finished. This finish, I surmised from Begaye's story-telling, sounded like the consequence of disconnections within Mother Earth, a severed core, empty of Earth's self.

Back under the Octagon, Begaye lifted the drum from the ground and placed it aside.

Without Indigenous values beautifully threading human activities into the weft of the Land, nothing holds the core together, they explained. The void left in the center was surrounded by a ring of children surrounded by a ring of women with an orbit of men behind them, having the others' backs, the backs of the outer ring exposed to outside the circle, beyond.

Begaye next asked the seated children to leave. Their departure, they explained, replayed the forced relegation of many of their grandparents and great-grandparents from their communities into distant boarding schools meant to assimilate them into English-speaking settler culture.[113]

"What's happening? Where are we going?" asked one child, distracted by a five-week-old puppy snuggling in their sweatshirt.

Then Begaye walked around the circle, tapping shoulders. First the women, then the men. The tapped ones stepped away. This reenacted the further erosion of many Indigenous communities via historic and ongoing traumas. These included settler-brought diseases, murders, and kidnappings – especially of missing girls and women. Forced sterilizations. The overuse of drugs and alcohol, suicides – especially by young men. Poisoned air and warming climate tied with stolen children, appropriated and looted lands, alienation from ancestral land-valuing responsibilities, prohibited songs, stifled language, ruthless assimilation into a foreign tongue, forbidden country foods, shackled values and fragmented knowledge systems, shattered identities, griefs over lost loved ones.[114]

As the circles broke apart, my throat contracted. I heard others quietly sobbing. This IS the end of the world. Words – "there is no core" – involuntarily, I felt, came out of my mouth.

Begaye brought us back together to talk a bit more. Then we all took a break.

---

[112] See also Guerra, C. and S. Guerra. (2019). *The Condor and the Eagle*, https://thecondorandtheeagle.com.

[113] Tanana Chiefs Conference. "Legacy of Our Elders: Luke Titus, Minto," https://www.tananachiefs.org/legacy-of-our-elders/.

[114] Native Movement, Crawl Walk Run, and the University of Alaska Fairbanks, et al. (2017). *We Breathe Again*, www.nativemovement.org/we-breathe-again-film.

I walked slowly to the river and dipped my fingers into one small eddy. I heard the frontlines echo – "water is life."

The representation of Mother Earth's connective core by a drum felt carefully chosen. In positive decolonizing inversion – now the restless songs awake, Begaye encouraged. And Native languages lead Indigenous Peoples back. Speaking her welcome in reclaimed Iñupiatun, Siqiñiq Maupin, co-founder and first director of Sovereign Iñupiat for a Living Arctic (www.silainuat.org), spoke of "Iñupiaq values." "It is respect for nature," they said, "respect for others, and our sacred relationship with the bowhead whale, with our tuttu, is something that I work really hard to bring to the surface again, because it's sleeping, that relationship." Maupin urged that it is time to wake up and reconnect and protect what is left, while "we can still change, and we can still get our animals to be healthy again." They entreated with a caution. "But if we continue to go down the path that we know is not right in our hearts we're going to see changes that are irreversible and that's what pushes me" (Gwich'in Steering Committee, 2020: 44–45).[115]

Within community, as Maupin helped me hear, many are healing back into the millennia-long old-new adaptive legacy of ancestral relationships in Arctic lifescapes broken by outsiders. It is not as if they are evolving toward some land ethic that Iñupiat and other relations had never had.

For me, as a Euro-American-settler trained in Leopoldian conservation, to be welcomed into this gathering of deep knowledge-sharing and feeling was a generosity that calls forth my own responsibility. I will/keep listening to learn how to be supportive in relations with Iñupiaq/t, Gwich'in, Diné, Tohono O'odham, and other Indigenous persons and Peoples on the way to Land and cultural rematriation and just and re/generative prosperity that somehow enmeshes all of us.

5.2 Indigenous Inheritance: Enacting Ecologies, Languages, Story

Leopold's ecological ethical vision projected a grand narrative of historical-evolutionary moral ascension that runs counter to many Indigenous stories of ethical-relational continuity with the Land. It also projected a manifest destiny project involving genocide, racist population control and/or eugenics as forms of appropriating land from future generations. Future generations, whether as dispossessed or unborn, could not "inherit" it. His sweeping narrative maintained relegation of Native Peoples into reservations (in Alaska, rather, a complex organization of for-profit corporations, villages, and urbanization).[116]

---

[115] Also Campbell, S., J. Manthei, and J. Warren. (2021). "Folk School, Aldo Leopold's Legacy: A Conversation," www.youtube.com/watch?v=B9iqfeDYzNs.

[116] Sullivan, M. (2022). "ANSCA," www.tananachiefs.org/wp-content/uploads/2022/05/ANCSA-a-complete-of-incomplete-story-of-tribal-governance.pdf.

It perpetuated the assimilative force, into ideal white epistemologies and other Euro-American ideals, of land allotment policies and child-imprisoning schools. Settler-colonial ideals echoed from supremacist culture in the vexingly contradictory land-ruining "progress" – with technological innovations outpacing ethical ones – which Leopold criticized. Those ideals echoed as well in conservation modes he helped invent intending to improve people.

Leopold proposed re-engineering the Euro-American population rather than recognize that eliminating Indigenous Peoples – from his models and from their homelands – continued deepening rather than bridging the problematic "gap" between land misuse and ethical human culture. Conservation, including Leopoldian conservation, as well as profit-driven industry, albeit with crucial differences, involved destruction in order to rebuild colonial forms of desire. As Noah Schlager put it, white settler conservation and its still-influential Leopoldian legacy embedded a violently anti-Indigenous narrative from the start –"a forest without Indians is better than a forest with Indians, which is better than a barren mountainside." Without questioning white supremacist and colonialist power structures – Leopoldian models of change, intended for good – would continue reinscribing on-the-ground oppressions of Indigenous Peoples, racialized Black and Brown people, especially women, LGBTQIA+ and/or disabled persons, children, and/or even white people deemed merely "mass-minded" or "average."

At a Bureau of Land Management [BLM] hearing in Fairbanks in winter 2019, Indigenous persons – including Gwich'in, Iñupiaq, and Ahtna – voiced deep knowledge of all-too-familiar settler-colonial logic and duplicity. This logic was ingrained not only within the BLM's resource-based, intergenerational mission promising to sustain "the health, diversity, and productivity of public lands."[117] It also was instilled in many conservationists' desire to conserve land even in less utilitarian-extractive ways and in more Leopoldian ones, that is, as wilderness protectors. Many such conservationists wished to stand as allies with many Alaska Native persons against oil extraction in their customary lands. Settler-conservationists desiring to be allies may be thinking we have important ethics in common with Alaska Native people yet would do well to learn how to listen for important differences, so as not to reinscribe the racist and colonial fracture by continuing to tend only the environmental one, thus failing to mend each and together. Against the backdrop of U.S. bureaucracy, most, if not all, of the Alaska Native speakers, for example, were expressing their own Peoples' determinations to defend their ancestral geographies in their own terms; to keep their own long-enacted cultural norms,

---

[117] The Bureau of Land Management, "Home," www.blm.gov.

including sciences; to honor their own ecologies of relations and facilitate their own collective continuances in customary lands, including their own languages, often incommensurable with English-word understandings like "resource," "conservation," "refuge," and/or "wilderness."

"I talk from my heart," said Neets'aii Gwich'in Elder Dr. Sarah James. This hearing was specifically focused on oil and gas leasing in Iizhik Gwats'an Gwandaii Goodlit, the Sacred Place Where Life Begins. This coastal plain – land never ceded to any colonial government – is the Porcupine Caribou Herd calving ground, which Gwich'in themselves know how to keep from disturbing, even by their own presence. Porcupine Caribou, at their calving post, nursing and training ground, "want quiet, clean, private where they can have their calf." That is what she wanted when she had her child – "for him." "And that goes for all life," she said (BLM, 2019a: 6; BLM, 2023: 27–30). The flourishing of Gwich'in and vadzaih (Porcupine Caribou) is integrated spiritually, nutritionally, and culturally, as it has been for millennia, for time immemorial (Gwich'in Steering Commitee, 2020: 4). The U.S. calls this caribou birthing area the 1002 area, which is embedded in its 1980-designated nineteen (plus)-million acre Arctic National Wildlife Refuge. When James spoke at the 2019 Fairbanks hearing, she noted that the government had not mapped "our subsistence use area" correctly. Speaking in English, James explained, she was speaking in her "second language." Since colonization, she stressed, "We can only be gone so much from the village or Western life in order to make it in two world [sic]." Their children, James explained, are expected to respect their elders, land, and language and then also go out to get their "higher education." "Our people are living in two world [sic]," she stressed (BLM, 2019a: 29–42).

In the colonialists' world, the U.S.-designated Refuge contains the second largest area of designated wilderness – some eight million acres. In the words of the 1964 federal Wilderness Act defining it, this is a place wherein "the earth and its community of life are untrammeled by man, where man himself is a visitor who does not remain."[118] At the northern boundary of the Arctic Refuge, outside this vast wilderness area, is one and a half million acres of coastal plain. The plain is a relatively narrow band, sheltering the caribou calving nursery, between the Brooks Range and the Arctic Ocean. Some industry politicians believe this area will become lucrative, viewing Alaska as a vast "natural resource" warehouse, so vast that such a little drilling can't hurt, they claim.[119] Some conservationists are

---

[118] U.S. 88th Congress, Second Session. (September 3, 1964). "The Wilderness Act, Public Law 88-577 (16 U.S.C. 1131-1136),"https://wilderness.net/learn-about-wilderness/key-laws/wilderness-act/default.php.

[119] Downing, S. (2017). "ANWR Is a Dot on Don Young's Nose," https://mustreadalaska.com/anwr-dot-don-youngs-nose/. In 2019, Don Young claimed Gwich'in were not People he

fighting for it to become additional wilderness within the Refuge, a stronger protection against extraction. With obviously crucial differences, nonetheless, in each case, the land is a sort of blank space whose use non-Alaska Native decision-makers – that is, the BLM in an oil v wilderness tug of war – might presume to make. Meanwhile, in 2017, Alaska Senator Lisa Murkowski bypassed transparent legislative channels and surreptitiously attached a coastal plain drilling mandate, Public Law 115–97, to the Tax Cuts and Jobs Act, which passed. This Public Law 115–97 presented the most urgent threat since 1988, when the Gwich'in Nation united in defense of Iizhik Gwats'an Gwandaii Goodlit.[120]

In 1988, Gwich'in elders had called for a feast bringing together all their Tribes, separated by U.S. and Canadian government boundaries, for the first time in a century. In James's words, her Nation was taking "a position as a people of the land as they did before our first visitor came to our area." Gwich'in have gathered every two years since in defense of the Porcupine Caribou Herd, which – because they are so interwoven – is also a defense of the Gwich'in themselves. The elders guided the Nation to form the Gwich'in Steering Committee [GSC], which is directed with that prime purpose. As James, an original GSC spokesperson, highlighted, it was "like a dream, reunited, like birth of a nation – reunited birth of a nation like we always happen before the border" (BLM, 2019a: 7). And because "oil is huge," as James often says, the GSC also works to educate white people about Gwich'in connection to the caribou and their inherent right to continue their way of life (BLM, 2019a, 8; Fairbanks Public Hearing, 2023, personal communication; Dunaway, 2021: 109, see Mishler and Frank, 2019).

In 2012 and, again, in 2022, the Gwich'in Nation unanimously passed Gwich'in Niintsyaa, their "Resolution to Protect the Birthplace and Nursery

---

represented, to which Gwich'yaa Zhee Gwich'in 2nd Chief, Sam Alexander, took over the floor: www.youtube.com/watch?v=0Yq1DkXr6c8

[120] The fight against this threat goes on to date. See Gwich'in Steering Committee, "News," https://ourarcticrefuge.org/c/news/; Dunaway, F. (2023). *Defending the Arctic Refuge: A Book and Public History Site*, https://defendingthearcticrefuge.com/additional_sources/; U.S. Federal Register (September 8, 2023). "Notice of Availability of the Draft Coastal Plain Oil and Gas Leasing Program Supplemental Environmental Impact Statement," www.federalregister.gov/documents/2023/09/08/2023-19427/notice-of-availability-of-the-draft-coastal-plain-oil-and-gas-leasing-program-supplemental. In 2023, Senators Markey, Cantwell, Heinrich, and Bennet and Representatives Huffman and Fitzpatrick reintroduced the Arctic Refuge Protection Act, www.markey.senate.gov/news/press-releases/markey-huffman-fitzpatrick-reintroduce-bipartisan-legislation-to-protect-the-arctic-refuge. Gwich'in Tribes asked the Biden administration to establish an Indigenous sacred site in the coastal plain, which did not happen before he left office in 2025 (DeMarban, A. (2024). "Biden administration weighs establishing sacred Indigenous site in Arctic refuge after request from tribes," *Anchorage Daily News*, www.adn.com/business-economy/energy/2024/10/16/biden-administration-weighs-establishing-sacred-indigenous-site-in-arctic-refuge-after-request-from-tribes/). A second lease sale, in early January 2025, required under the tax mandate resulted in zero bids.

Grounds of the Porcupine Caribou Herd." This was an announcement "in black and white" to the "outside world" – made, again, as James put it, because "we can't do it by ourself. We can't because oil is huge" (BLM, 2019a: 8). With a united voice against extractors, the Gwich'in Nation reaffirmed their resolve to defend "the inherent right to continue our way of life" against what is ongoing colonialism. As they note in Gwich'in Niintsyaa, this is a right "recognized and affirmed by Article 1 of the International Covenant of Civil and Political Rights, ratified by the U.S. Senate, and reads in part: *In no case may a People be deprived of their own means of <u>subsistence</u>*" (underline mine). This 2022 Gwich'in statement also concluded by resolving "that the 1002 area of the Arctic National Wildlife Refuge be made *Wilderness* [italics mine] by the U.S. Government to protect *Iizhik Gwats'an Gwandaii Goodlit* (The Sacred Place Where Life Begins) for generations to come."[121]

The document announced all of this for English speakers, and with their Nation's children so recently punished for speaking their own language. The Anglo-American colonizers also had "renamed" vast areas of Gwich'in, Iñupiat, and other Alaska Native traditional lands enacting linguistic relegation and geographical appropriation within a colonial extraction-protection framework. With generations of forced assimilation and disruption of kinship relations, probably only three hundred persons – most over fifty-five – speak semi-/fluent Dinjii Zhuh ginjìk (Dinjii Zhuh k'yàa), a "severely endangered" language (Mishler and Frank, 2019: 34). Yet, by their communities' intensive care, resurgent.[122]

Another speaker who testified at the Fairbanks hearing also focused on language and translation – particularly on the incommensurability of meanings with very real, incommensurable consequences. Shawna Larson, a younger woman who is Sugpiaq (Port Graham) on her mother's side and Ahtna (Chickaloon) on her father's, first emphasized: "We support the Gwich'in People." She added, "Those are our relatives. We support the Porcupine Caribou Herd." "We heard a lot of the elders talking about how there is no way to express certain things in their own traditional language,"

---

[121] The Gwich'in Nation. (2022). Gwich'in Niintsyaa, https://trustees.org/wp-content/uploads/2022/07/RES-Gwichin-Niintsyaa_PASSED_22Jul19.pdf ; https://defendingthearcticrefuge.com/additional_sources/; A historic film is Gwich'in Steering Committee/G. Henry and R. Carroll/Yukon Native Broadcasting. (1999). *Gwich'in Niintsyaa 1988,* www.youtube.com/watch?v=oLdEOdh5pA8.

[122] GTC Department of Cultural Heritage: Gwich'in Social and Cultural Institute. "How We Speak," www.gwichin.ca/how-we-speak; Gwich'in Tribal Council, "Language Revitalization: Language Nest Project," www.gwichintribal.ca/language-revitalization.html, Dinjii Zhuh Ginjik (Alaskan Gwich'in Language) Online Dictionary, https://dictionary.gwichinlanguage.org; Johnson, P. D. and A. Carlson. (2022). "Diiyeghan naii Taii Tr'eedaa (We Will Walk the Trail of Our Ancestors)," www.reciprocity.org/films/diiyeghan-naii-taii-treedaa.

Larson continued. "There is no way to say it, really, in English" (BLM, 2019b: 85–87).[123]

Larson then unfolded a story, which I share with her consent, of how her traditional tribal council elders had asked her to help find a better English word than "subsistence" to describe their way of life. Because, Larson explained, the dictionary meaning is "to merely survive." "We are not merely surviving. We are thriving and we are living. We have a relationship with the land," she emphasized. So Larson turned to other elders to ask how to say this in English. Trying to convey what she meant, Larson held up one hand to represent "this is the land and the animals" and the other to represent "this is the People." She clasped her hands together and then asked them, "in our language, how do you say this?" One elder now responded, "Oh, oh, oh, oh. You can't. There is no one word for that." He told her,

> That's why we have stories. Stories make you feel. And what you are describing is a relationship. And that's the only way you can really know what and how you are interacting with the land and with the animals and with each other.

"We had these also, stories about our relationship with the animals," Larson concluded her comment, "and it just makes me realize, a Westernized colonial view, world view, cannot be translated into an Indigenous world view. It just can't" (BLM, 2019b: 85–87).

Vásquez-Fernández and Ahenakew pii tai poo taa (2020) support the awkwardness of a word like "subsistence" considered in the BLM hearing. "Sustainable" and "development" combined, for example, as they detail, are merely other terms for ongoing paradigms of colonial disrespect and exploitation as usual. Listening to this, listening to Larson, James and so many others as a rejoinder to the domination of Leopoldian and other settler concepts is to keep deepening reflections on how "subsistence," as well as "conservationist," "environmentalist," "wilderness," and many other English words – words that Anglos so often expect Indigenous speakers to use – might not be translatable into their own ethical and knowledge systems (Dunaway 2021: 108, 166).[124] Perhaps the same goes for "land use," "gap," "human culture," and (ethical) "bridge."

In Gwich'in Niintsyaa, the Gwich'in Nation resolved, in English, on protecting their "subsistence," linked with "human rights," and used the term

---

[123] Story shared with Larson's consent, Personal email, 5-13-22. Thank you, again, Shawna.
[124] Demientieff, B. (2020). "What Will It Take," www.newyorker.com/news/annals-of-a-warming-planet/what-will-it-take-to-cool-the-planet; Harball, E. (2019). "We're never going to surrender," https://alaskapublic.org/2019/07/17/sarah-james-on-a-life-fighting-oil-drilling-in-the-arctic-refuge/.

"wilderness" in defense of their way of life. Does the term "wilderness" translate into what Gwich'in mean by Iizhik Gwats'an Gwandaii Goodlit? (Whyte 2014: 3; Gilio-Whitaker, 2019: 145; Warren, 2024). And if not, how could it *not* somehow mean to model different systems of land ethics and practices? Does "ethic" itself have a commensurable Gwich'in meaning, and/or are there multiple conceptions that I might not be able to grasp? Recall how Whyte described the Anishinaabe women elders' Mother Earth Water Walk – the aspects of interspecies reciprocity and social justice – in contrast with what Leopold modeled as a settler land conservationist. Moreover, as much as I lean in to respect the way Demientieff knows the heart of her People, herself, and Vadzaih as part of each other, how could my relations with that place be anything like hers? How could any inheritance fractured in colonial and environmental terms and transmitted over a matter of single digit generations be commensurate with Indigenous rights and responsibilities lived out over time immemorial? "*Indigenous* is a birthright word," Robin Kimmerer writes (2013: 213). Recall what we hear when respected Neets'aii Gwich'in Trimble Gilbert of Vashraii K'oo (Arctic Village) talks of his Gwich'in worldview describing appropriate relationships pre-existing colonization, that is, as a way of life, self-determining, "long before his homeland was overlain with the Western refuge-wilderness ideology." For him, the "Refuge," that is, Iizhik Gwats'an Gwandaii Goodlit, is "'the land that holds the bones of thousands of generations of my ancestors.'"[125]

A third woman, following and followed by many others, has called "Gwich'in" the "language of my soul" (Long, 2017). Caroline Tritt-Frank, from Vashraii K'oo, is a language teacher. "I think if they [oil and gas extractors] interfere with the caribou," she explained, "that will destroy their [the children's] language, their way of talking because everything that they use on caribou is used in Gwich'in. And so every single piece of the caribou has a Gwich'in name." And this is what is passed on by elders who "usually speak about hunting." "So," she said, "I think the language is a major concern for me and the caribou that the elders live on" (BLM, 2019b: 41–3; Mishler and Frank, 2019).

As I listened closely to the Alaska Native persons at this BLM hearing – I understood that they would never give up courageously defending something that did not translate into "subsistence." It did not sound to me like "natural resources" nor defenses of Leopoldian "wilderness," either, in Ybarra's words, land that "sits there with its soul hollowed out, emptied of the peoples who help

---

[125] Kaye, R., P.N. Andrews, and B. Demientieff (2021). "Wilderness and Traditional Indigenous Beliefs," https://rewilding.org/wilderness-and-traditional-indigenous-beliefs-conflicting-or-intersecting-perspectives-on-the-human-nature-relationship/.

animate the land" (2022: 35).[126] These terms sounded like the currently most apt yet still inadequate conservation "tools" for overturning colonialist domination and liberating "Indigenous conceptions of relationality" (Gilio-Whitaker, 2019: 145).[127] They sounded like "sites of interaction," in Whyte's words (2014: 3). What I heard at the hearing sounded to me like the antithesis of Indigenous relegation, appropriation, and assimilation. It seemed to belong to desired abolitionist futures. I heard it sounding more like decolonization, like Land Back, like rematriated sovereignty and Peoples at liberty to make and keep up their own land-ethical relationships, their responsibilities. It sounded like Whyte's "collective continuance." Riffing on Schlager's thesis in reverse, maybe I was hearing a narrative something like: Indigenous sovereignty in sacred Lands without a U.S. federal wilderness designation is better than a wilderness designation, which is better than extraction like oil and gas drilling. Maybe it sounded something like everything – past, present, future – in Peoples' own tongues. Maybe, attuning with Larson's testimony, it meant Indigenous Peoples' own ongoing stories.

5.3 Indigenous Epistemological Privilege: There's a Story (Not an Allegory)

In "The Land Ethic," Leopold whited out "Indians" from "The Biotic Pyramid," which he envisioned as an apt "symbol of land." "Wilderness," too, as a norm, placed Black persons, Indigenous persons and sovereign Nations, intersecting with disabled persons and/or those having class-imposed limits outside the land-ethical practices focused on land health. These proposals also demeaned these "others," placing them – with their languages, systems of knowledge production, and ethics – outside the bounds of a supposedly more supreme human capacity for thinking, ethical agency, and technological innovation. Leopold's eliminations – all with very real on-the-ground anti-Indigenous consequences – also could discredit Leopold's common concept of land, as thus based in biased evidence, calling into question ethics and sciences reliant on it.

Aldo Leopold's Odyssey has ambiguous meanings, as I have mentioned. One of its facets is an essay by Leopold titled "Odyssey." That essay, like "Song of the Gavilan," brings alive Leopold's "land pyramid" from "The Land Ethic,"

---

[126] In 2019, the U.S. House passed "H.R. 1146 Arctic Cultural and Coastal Plain Protection Act," sponsored by Rep Jared Huffman (D-CA-2), www.congress.gov/bill/116th-congress/house-bill/1146. Reintroduced in 2023 (fn118), it would "amend PL 115-97 ... to repeal the Arctic National Wildlife Refuge oil and gas program." It does not refer to "wilderness."

[127] Also IMAGO Initiative. (2023). "Reimagining Conservation Through an Indigenous Lens," The Wilderness Society at, www.wilderness.org/key-issues/wildlands-everyone/imago-initiative.

which is "a fountain of energy flowing through a circuit of soils, plants and animals," including "man" (1949: 215). As we have seen, this normative image is faulty as "man" means settlers (and does indeed also privilege men). In his "Odyssey," Leopold portrays complex ecological dependencies in an efficiently told story about two nutrient atoms. Each atom takes a contrasting ecological trip through the "[prairie] world of living things" before and after the pioneers become wheat farmers there (1949: 104). These latter clearly need to ascend along the land ethical path. At the same time, as in others of Leopold's works, there is a generic "Indian." In this tale, the Indigenous person receives and redistributes nutrient atoms before becoming replaced. Inheriting "the eagle's plumes," with them, he "propitiated the Fates." While the essentials of Leopold's knowledge in "Odyssey," if not cause-and-effect itself, apparently do not "occur to him" (106). This person sounds like a spiritual animal, if human, yet not one capable of scientific nor land-ethical thinking.

On the other hand, in "Song of the Gavilan," "the old Indian" Leopold refers to seems to have been capable of good land relations, but is already a ghost himself, mythic and unthreatening (Leopold, 1949: 149–154). In this narrative, retaining previously noted attitudes, including to Paiute, Apache, and Pueblo Peoples, Leopold takes up the now-vacated role of hunter within his "symbolic structure," hunter, as if, even now as an adult, Leopold is "playing Indian" (Deloria, 2022, 107).[128] "The structure [of the scene] is symbolic." "Food is the continuum." "Food is the continuum" flooded by the energy of "sunshine" in an ecological dreamscape in which he belongs. Meanwhile, Leopold fears that other settlers, with powerful tools but more rudimentary ethics, will arrive with their notions of scientific progress and destroy the community's healthful functioning (1949: 153–154). Leopold thus paints himself as a hunter superior both to Indigenous persons and to average settlers by virtue of being driven by more than the hunger of subsistence living, on the one hand, or profit-driven utility, on the other. This sport hunter whom he self-represents, presumably with a fine racial inheritance of wildlife interest, has knowingly exchanged a more certain venison meal for ethical self-limitation. Finally, Leopold evokes Judeo-Christian biblical terms for his rightful homecoming into an existentially alluring scene – "Dust to dust, stone age to stone age, but always the eternal chase!" (1949: 151).

At the Climate Summit in Gwich'yaa Zhee, for the first time, I witnessed Native experts – including elders and traditional hunters, some additionally trained in dominant, big S science – hosting academic non-Native scientists.

---

[128] As boyhood is for "Daniel-Booneing" and – as "ontogeny repeats phylogeny" for individuals, society, and race – the more mature adult plays at Indigenous replacement? (1949: 175–178).

The gathering conveyed a powerful alternative to white privilege and Indigenous suppression. Darrell Vent, of Huslia, along the Koyukuk River, told how the Central Arctic caribou herd was split by the Trans-Atlantic Pipeline in the 1970s despite federal agents promising otherwise. This is a story of great concern, too, as more extraction in Iizhik Gwats'an Gwandaii Goodlit threatens the Porcupine Herd. "We had to adapt to what they did . . . but we can't hunt in our area . . . they [the Central Herd] moved away," Vent said. And now hunters must travel 70–120 air miles distant. "And its not as good [fat] as the caribou we used to get," Vent continued. Our people, he said, had to adapt, have always had to adapt in different ways and have done so from "a long time ago." Now they have "started hunting more for moose, fish, other species," Vent continued. At the same time, with layers of challenges adding up fast, "because of global warming we're seeing that the moose is having a tougher time to survive" (Gwich'in Steering Committee, 2020: 34–35). And as Gwich'in hunter Chuck Peter observed, "There's these 'specklebellies' . . . White-fronted geese," also important food, and ". . . this heat, the sun, it's driving them up north faster." "Soon as the river goes, boom they're gone," Peter reported. If life depends on food security, food security depends on discerning and adapting to changes in the land community. "We got to risk our lives . . . cause we gotta fight with the icebergs in the channel breaking up," Peter explained. Moreover, "Our [Yukon] river is drying up . . . the water is changing," King salmon and other fish are suffering followed by fishing restrictions with grave impacts. "I just wanted to mention how important that King Salmon is," Peter stressed (Gwich'in Steering Committee, 2020: 18). Gwich'in elder Stephen Frost, Sr. told the gathered group, "I've seen all the changes . . . All the permafrost going . . . I'll do more listening, but later on maybe I might find my way to talk again" (32).[129]

Bernadette Demientieff often has stressed, "My elders are my scientists. They have warned us that this [oil and gas drilling] is not a good idea."[130] The Vuntut Gwitchin, across the imposed U.S.-Canada border in Old Crow, have issued the first known Indigenous declaration of climate emergency, "Yeendoo Diinehdoo Ji'heezrit Nits'oo Ts'o' Nan He'aa," or "After Our Time, How Will the World Be." This pivotal declaration emphasizes that "Indigenous peoples and local Arctic, coastal and agricultural communities have vast and unique knowledge systems, practices and technologies for

---

[129] For more understanding of the critical situation and responses, see Woods, B., L. Heller, M. Quillen, J. Howard, et al. Indigenizing Salmon Fisheries in Alaska, https://storymaps.arcgis.com/stories/and43ae5f7ae3b84a85889e7b8ada4561f0 ; Native Movement. Gath and K'iyh: Listening to Heal With Cellist Yo-Yo-Ma, https://www.nativemovement.org/nm-blog/2023/9/18/gath-amp-kiyh-listen-to-heal-with-cellist-yo-yo-ma.

[130] (2020): 6.; Rothko Chapel Oscar Romero Award Ceremony. (2020), https://vimeo.com/136731614.

"Alaska" Is Not a Blank Space 103

mitigating and adapting to the impacts of climate change as the worlds' most environmentally conscious inhabitants." It affirms "the imperative that Indigenous peoples be central to every effort for mitigating and adapting to climate change at local to international scales."[131]

At another land protection event, the young Vuntut Chief (of Old Crow, a Gwich'in village on the other side of the current U.S. Canada border), thirty-one-year-old Dana Tizya-Tramm, shared a story "that puts all of this in focus," he said. This, along with the following, I share with his consent.[132] The elder's story helps explain how "there's a lot more to these lands than oil and gas." "We were driving up the river and going up to [the elder's] camp," Tizya-Tramm shared,

> And we passed a moose. And as we turned the corner going around the next bend in the river, he told me, "you saw that moose?" And I told him, "yeah." And he said, "that moose has been there my whole life." And we kept going. And I thought about it. And right away that moose looked no more than four or five years old. And I thought, what does he mean, "his whole life," he's an elder?
>
> But as I really began to unpack it, I realized what he was saying – that, that creek has always had moose in it. And, later on when we got to the camp, he said, 'don't bother that creek and the moose will always be there.[133]

In Tizya-Tramm's story I hear that the moose was really there. The elder was really there. He, himself, was really there. Their ancestors' bodies were in that ground. And future generations would be born there, coming and going, and passing along the river. "It's actually all of us in there together," Tizya-Tramm said.

Then, in another breath, "it's hard to sit down with some of the staffers or representatives or others in oil and gas industry that look at the pure economic side of things." "And this," Tizya-Tramm continued, "is where rationality has an ability to pop in when it's us versus them," which he could not see in that way. Seeing land only economically, in terms of oil and gas, "in my view," Tizya-Tramm stressed, "I actually find a misappropriation of what the term *energy* truly is." This is what the elder's story put into focus, he explained:

---

[131] Vuntut Gwitchen First Nation Council. (2010). Yeendoo Diinehdoo Ji'heezrit Nits'oo Ts'o' Nan He'aa, www.vgfn.ca/pdf/CC%202019%20Declaration.pdf; Gwich'in Council International. (2018). *Impact Assessment in the Arctic: Emerging Practices of Indigenous-led Review*, https://gwichincouncil.com/impact-assessment-arctic; Holland, E. (2019). "Bringing Old Crow to the World," https://uphere.ca/articles/bringing-old-crow-world.

[132] Stories shared by consent, personal email, 5-2-2022. Thank you, again, Chief Dana Tizya-Tramm.

[133] Tizya-Tramm, D. (2018). "The Truth About Seismic," last accessed 2020, www.nativemovement.org/enviro-justice.

When you go into this area [Iizhik Gwats'an Gwandaii Goodlit], as fragile as it is, and a keystone in the arctic ecosystems – and, you go, and you drill there – yes, you can get your oil out of there, if there's anything significant in there. But what you are sacrificing is a different perspective on energy because these [Porcupine Herd] caribou go to this area.

And, by the way, they are the last healthy herd of caribou right across all Canada. All caribou are historically in decline. And, this is the last healthy herd, the largest land animal migration in the world.

And they convert lichens and cottongrasses and different foods into nutrients that they lock into their bodies. And, they move across our lands delivering these nutrients to the Gwich'in Nation, the Indigenous Peoples, and to the bears and to the wolves. And they drive this huge, ancient ecosystem in which we are tied to.

And that is now being threatened without recourse or some actual tools to have some real considerations and some meaningful conversations on a level that will truly express the actual importance of this area (2018).

To me, at least at first, it *sounds like* both Leopold's biotic pyramid and Tizya-Tramm's tellings mean similar things. Both seem to be imagining intergenerational hunts and flows of nutrients and energy through ecosystems. When I first heard Tizya-Tramm's stories, I felt myself pulled toward an assumption of common ground between settler and Gwich'in ways and understandings, veering toward what Whyte warns of as a "convergence view." Yes, I felt a definite pull. I also felt the tug of my old colonizer habit of passing what I heard Tizya-Tramm say through the filter of what I thought I already knew, what Whyte warns of as a "translational view." That pull was toward expectations for a Gwich'in perspective to be evaluated and legitimized according to my cultural ancestor's rules. And then, I resisted.

Here are some ways I resist. I remember how Leopold's writings and my uncritical scholarship were not only extraneous but also offensive to many Alaska Native and other Indigenous, Black, and Chicanx members of my community, and how I felt when I learned that. I recall Harrison's suggestion that listeners can neither avow nor refuse and reciprocally rejoinder an ancestral proposal if they have either failed to hear it or do not understand the language in which the proposal is made. In the latter case, this may be a sort of refusal to/of the listeners, in the sense that Iñupiat words in Joan Naviyuk Kane's "Exceeding Beringia" interrupt the expectation of English censoring the poem to non-Iñupiat outsiders (Smith, 2021: 168). I hear Larson, echoing her elders: "There is no way to say it, really, in English." I don't forget James saying, "oil is huge" and "we can't do it by ourself." And also, I hear her say, "We're huge" – Gwich'in, allied Alaska Native Groups, and more whom Gwich'in have educated since 1988 (BLM, 2019a, 37). I gratefully show up for trainings by Gwich'in about Gwich'in connection to the caribou and salmon and support them in defending their rightful way of life. I ask if this or that word or deed will *not* ultimately reproduce relationships of colonial domination, as Gilio-Whitaker prompts. I remember McLean suggesting that if there was a history before race/ism, there is one afterwards. I rehearse Rodríguez's warning against a so-called practical, normalized "common sense" that would obstruct what is necessary to undermine (carceral) totalizing logics. I open to the dreaming of disabled lands and bodies, as Tsaplina suggests. I deepen my hearing of Whyte's rejoinder to settler-colonialism – that is, "to respect differences and the possibility that non-Indigenous conversants will not immediately understand what all the issues may be, no matter how well they think they grasp the premises of the ethic to which they are trying to compare their own ethic." I hear Dotson's prompts – to keep *in focus* the structural "settler-native-slave triad" that keeps privileging the colonizing system. I recall Ybarra underscoring how Chicana feminists and many others have not needed white conservationists' teachings when they can keep learning from/with/as "those who embody survival and defiance" and "who have been able to endure for thousands of years." I keep relearning how to deeply and responsibly listen in something like Robinson's positionally responsible "panacoustic terms" acknowledging that not everything is for me. I strive to listen not only for avowable commonalities but also for differences – "intercultural equivocality" in Vásquez-Fernández's and Ahenakew's words – between my cultural ancestral claims to land ethics, land health, sustainability, and just climate action proposals, and those of Gwich'in and Black people/s, Chicanx, and anyone on the frontlines of structural oppressions. This unsettling and attuning to re-tune is necessary for any chance of genuine and durable coalitions between "people of all heritages," in Whyte's terms, so crucial to multiple desired futures. This is merely a beginning. And finally, I feel the warning of Ruiz and Dotson not to mistake a coalition for a home.

6 Conclusion: Toward Kinship

"Nanabozho" is the name of Creator's "First Man," "the last of all beings to be created," in Anishinaabeg storytelling, Robin Kimmerer shares with her readers (2013: 205). Perhaps, I wonder, to help Nanabozho refuse the great hoarder, Windigo, the medicine teachers of the North, "gave him *Wiingaashk.*" The teachers gifted Sweetgrass to Nanabozho "to teach him the ways of compassion, kindness, and healing, even for those who have made bad mistakes, for who has not?" (212). The generosity of Kimmerer's story-sharing is stunning and, likewise, challenging. "Can settlers be trusted to follow Nanabozho," she asks, "to walk so that 'each step is a greeting to Mother Earth?'" Kimmerer herself struggles with "grief and fear" who "still sit in the shadows, behind the glimmer of hope." "Together," she acknowledges, "they try to hold my heart closed." "But I need to remember," she continues, "that the grief is the settlers' as well." For instance, "They can't drink the water either" (211–212).

Perhaps, Kimmerer suggests to settlers, listen to "White Man's Footstep," "the common plantain" who came with us to "Turtle Island." This plant is also "a foreigner, an immigrant, but after five hundred years of living as a good neighbor, people forget that kind of thing" (213–214). Her generosity continues: "Plantain is not indigenous but 'naturalized.'" We colonialists might "strive to become naturalized to place." Again, to become naturalized "is to live as if this is the land feeds you ... to know that your ancestors lie in this ground ... to live as if your children's future matters, to take care of the land as if our lives and the lives of all our relatives depend on it. Because they do" (214–215)." Can "Second Man," following "Nanabozho's footsteps," even if not given to be "indigenous," Kimmerer asks, "nevertheless enter into the deep reciprocity that renews the world?"(213). To become Indigenous as her Citizen Potawatomi Nation has long grown to be, "is to grow the circle of healing to include all of Creation" (212). "Where are the stories that lead the way?" (207). With "time as a circle," as "Nanabozho's people know" (206), perhaps any willing Indigenous teachers can help re/orient the unsettling newcomers to someplace more like home. Perhaps we first will learn how to listen, attune with, and activate social justice without which land healing and affection will be most unlikely to achieve.

Many Indigenous Peoples have been cut out of Lands for centuries, reminds Kim Tallbear.[134] "The Original Instructions," writes Kimmerer, "have gotten tattered along the way and many have been forgotten" (207). Or in the activity shared through Enei Begaye in Gwich'yaa Zhee, the core may be empty.

I think about the circle's core, different pieces of Earth-into whole, healing as Siqiñiq Maupin reconnects with tuttu and Iñupiatun. "'Shalak naii!'" Everyone should learn that term 'Shalak naii!'" says Princess Daazhraii Johnson, speaking Dinjii Zhuh K'yàa at that 2019 Climate Summit. "'Shalak naii!'" she translates, helpfully, if not commensurably, into English, is "'My relations!' You're all my relations. That includes that river, the Yukon River," she says (Gwich'in Steering Committee, 2020: 29; see also Hausdoerffer et al., 2021: 100–109).

---

[134] Tallbear, K. (2020). "A Sharpening of the Already-Present," https://ehc.english.ucsb.edu/?p=20907%20with%20live%20discussion,%20https://www.youtube.com/watch?v=vdTqqzRsMFU.

"You know, we all make mistakes," Johnson continues, speaking to the self-governing "Gwich'in way," "but when we have a community that loves us...if you have a community that loves you, you know you can stand back up" (2020: 29). "We are Gwich'in people that never give up. We must stand together and go forward no matter what is happening around us," says Gwich'yaa Zhee Tribal Government First Chief Nancy James, while also welcoming everyone gathered, including non-Indigenous persons (11). The frame expands beyond humans and also across generations. "Our ancestors ... they told us not to get away from their guideline of survival. They said don't forget their name, don't forget – their way .... The caribou is the one that taught them how to survive," shares Gwich'in (Venetie and Arctic Village) elder, scholar, and storyteller Kenneth Drizhuu Frank (BLM, 2019b: 44). And I hear Kim Tallbear remind, "Humans learn from non-humans," from daily relations (2020: 29:50, 33:59).

Perhaps from radical hope's frontlines new terms will arise, which could include unsettling settlers, learning first how to listen (and how not to), in reciprocally re/learning and re/imagining together with the release of "our minds, bodies, and lands," with Land Back, "realizing Indigenous liberation" (Native Movement, 2018) and abolition. This, again, points to the need for Euro-American settler participants to respectfully talk with and back to our ancestors regarding their proposals, for instance, Leopold, and "to decenter defenses of and apologies" for him, in Whyte's terms (2024). Moreover, for the overturning of dominating structures, it calls participants to deeply revision any still-woven assumptions of white supremacy – any impositions of colonialist "models of environmental stewardship," "historical trajectories of ethics," and ideas of privileging "interpretive frameworks," not to mention, an imperial nation state, or sweeping worldview. (Whyte, 2024; also Harrison, 2003; Tallbear, 2019; Gillo-Whitaker, 2019). Perhaps doing this work could lead, in Whyte's words, "people of all heritages" – with "more careful consideration of potential differences" (2015: 15; 2024) – into and even beyond stable-coalition building. Perhaps those joining could be on our way to good relations and to kin-making that empowers plurality while shoring up what we earthlings do share in common (Vásquez-Fernández and Ahenakew, 2020: 65–69; Kanngieser and Todd, 2020; Whyte, 2020).[135]

Shalak naii.

Learning this term "Shalak naii" might mean getting caught up in something not easy to walk away from. I also continue to hear my own cultural ancestors' voices – Aldo Leopold's, also dear-to-me Nina's – encouraging me "to stay in it."

---

[135] Tallbear, K. (2020). "On Reviving Kinship and Sexual Abundance: Interview with Ayana Young," https://forthewild.world/listen/kim-tallbear-on-reviving-kinship-and-sexual-abundance-157.

It might be, then, that Leopoldian idea of wilderness as "a single starting point" – a violent abstraction that never really has existed – could bring its earnest perpetrators, like myself, around to attuning, in humility, to hearing better – "Shalak naii"[136] – in searches to and from multiple starting points for achieving re/generative and purposeful life ways that are also skillfully loving and thus also just.

---

[136] I wish to draw attention, again, to the importance, for settlers, of taking care not to appropriate, take lightly, and/or, in any other way, misuse this or any Indigenous concept, words, and/or language. I wish to remind us to respectfully leave room for not understanding, no matter how much we think we might or wish to grasp full and deep meanings, for Gwich'in persons of "Shalak naii." Furthermore, for listening to Lakȟóta perspectives on "Mitákuye Oyás'iŋ" that "loosely translates to 'we are all related' or 'all my relatives,'" I wish to point the reader to Bordeaux, C., M.V. Bordeaux, and L. Long Soldier, curators. (2017-2018). *Responsibilities and Obligations: Understanding Mitákuye Oyás'iŋ*. Exhibited at Racing Magpie, Rapid City, SD, https://www.racingmagpie.org/mitakuye-oyasin-exhibit; and to this talk by Long Soldier in which she discusses their concerns and collaboration (beginning at minute 27): Long Soldier, L. (2020). Poem Present Reading. University of Chicago Program in Creative Writing, https://www.youtube.com/watch?v=8bhJSxNaeyQ.

References

Baldwin, D., M. Noodin, and B. Perley. (2018). Surviving the Sixth Extinction: American Indian Strategies for Life in the New World. In R. Grusin, ed., *After Extinction*. Minneapolis: University of Minnesota Press, pp. 201–234.

Ben-zvi, Y. (2007). Where Did Red Go? Lewis Henry Morgan's Evolutionary Inheritance and U.S. Racial Imagination. *The New Centennial Review* 7(2): 201–229.

BLM. (2019a). In the Matter of: Coastal Plain Oil and Gas Leasing Program Draft Environmental Impact Statement Public Meeting: One-on-one transcript: Fairbanks, Alaska, https://eplanning.blm.gov/public_projects/nepa/102555/168827/205471/Fairbanks_one-on-one_transcript_Feb._4_2019.pdf.

BLM. (2019b). Coastal Plain Oil and Gas Leasing Program Draft Environmental Impact Statement Public Meeting: Fairbanks, Alaska.

BLM. (2023). Coastal Plain Oil and Gas Leasing Program Draft Supplemental Environmental Impact Statement, Public Meeting, Fairbanks, Alaska, https://eplanning.blm.gov/public_projects/2015144/200492847/20109161/251009161/10)%2023-Oct-23_CP%20Draft%20SEIS%20FAIRBANKS%20PM_Transcript_508.pdf.

Boas, F. (1911). *The Mind of Primitive Man*. New York: Macmillan.

Brown, D. E. and N. B. Carmony, eds. (1995). *Aldo Leopold's Southwest*. Albuquerque: University of New Mexico Press.

Burkhart, B. (2019). *Indigenizing Philosophy through the Land*. Lansing: Michigan State University Press.

Callicott, J. B. (ed.) (1987). *Companion to a Sand County Almanac*. Madison: University of Wisconsin Press.

Callicott, J. B. and E. Freyfogle. (1999). *For the Health of the Land: Previously Unpublished Essays and Other Writings*. Washington: Island Press.

Catton, T. (1997). Inhabited Wilderness: Indians, Eskimos, and National Parks in Alaska. Albuquerque: University of New Mexico Press.

Colebrook, C. (2018). Lives Worth Living: Extinction, Persons, Disability. In R. Grusin, ed., *After Extinction*. Minneapolis: University of Minnesota Press, pp. 151–171.

Cook, A. and B. Sheehey. (2020). Metaphorical and Literal Groundings: Unsettling Groundless Normativity in Environmental Ethics. *Environmental Ethics* 42(4): 335–352.

Coulthard, G. and L. B. Simpson. (2016). Grounded Normativity/Place-Based Solidarity. *American Quarterly* 68(2): 249–255.

Cronon, W. (1996). The Trouble with Wilderness: Or, Getting Back to the Wrong Nature. *Environmental History* 1(1): 7–28, https://doi.org/10.2307/3985059.

Cryer, D. (2015). A Contradictory Ethos Sportsman Citizenship and Native Exclusion in Aldo Leopold's *Pine Cone*. *New Mexico Historical Review* 90(4): 498–508.

Davis, H. and Z. Todd. (2017). On the Importance of a Date, or Decolonizing the Anthropocene. *ACME: An International Journal for Critical Geographies* 16(4): 761–780.

Dawson, A., F. Longo, and Survival International. (2023). *Decolonize Conservation: Global Voices for Indigenous Self-determination, Land, and a World in Common*. Brooklyn: Common Notions.

Deloria, P. J. (2022). *Playing Indian*. New Haven: Yale University Press.

Demuth, B. (2019). *Floating Coast*. New York: Norton.

Denevan, W. M. (1992). The Pristine Myth: The Landscape of the Americas in 1492. *Annals of the Association of American Geographers* 82(3): 369–385.

Dotson, K. (2018). On the Way to Decolonization. *AlterNative* 14(3): 190–199.

Dunaway, F. (2021). *Defending the Arctic Refuge: A Photographer, an Indigenous Nation, and a Fight for Environmental Justice*. Chapel Hill: University of North Carolina Press.

Dunbar-Ortiz, R. (2014). *An Indigenous Peoples' History of the United States*. Boston: Beacon Press.

Dunn, S. W. (1994). *The Mohican and Their Land: 1609–1730*. Fleischmanns: Purple Mountain Press.

Eliot, T. S. (1943). *Four Quartets*. New York: Harcourt.

Estes, N. (2019). *Our History Is the Future: Standing Rock versus the Dakota Access Pipeline, and the Long Tradition of Indigenous Resistance*. London: Verso.

Ferdinand, M. (2022). *Decolonial Ecology: Thinking from the Caribbean World*. Medford: Polity Press.

Figueroa, J. (2024). *Mother Island: A Daughter Claims Puerto Rico*. New York: Pantheon Books.

Fix, A. J., H. Burnam, and R. Gutteriez. (2019). Toward Interspecies Thinking as a Collaborative Concept: Autoethnographies at the Intersection of Traditional Ecological Knowledge and Animal Studies. *HUMaNIMALIA* 10(2): 128–149.

Flader, S. (1994). *Thinking Like a Mountain*. Madison: University of Wisconsin.

Flader, S. L. (1991). Leopold on Wilderness. *American Forests*, 97(5–6): 32–33, 66–67.

Flader, S. L. and J. B. Callicott, eds. (1991). *The River of the Mother of God and Other Essays by Aldo Leopold.* Madison: University of Wisconsin Press.

Fleming, W. and W. Forbes. (2006). Following in Leopold's Footsteps: Revisiting and Restoring the Rio Gavilan Watershed. *Ecological Restoration* 24(1): 25–31.

Fuentes, A., R.R. Ackermann, and S. Athreya, et al. (2019). AAPA Statement on Race and Racism. *American Journal of Anthropology* 169: 400–402.

Galton, F. (1883, 2007, 2018). In G. Tredoux, ed., *Inquiries Into Human Faculty and Its Development.* First Electronic Edition, https://galton.org/books/human-faculty/index.html

Genetin-Pilawa, C. J. (2012). *Crooked Paths to Allotment: The Fight over Federal Indian Policy after the Civil War.* Chapel Hill: University of North Carolina Press.

Gilio-Whitaker, D. (2019). *As Long as Grass Grows: The Indigenous Fight for Environmental Justice from Colonization to Standing Rock.* Boston: Beacon Press.

Gilio-Whitaker, D. (2023). What Decolonizing Conservation Means and Why It Matters. In A. Dawson, F. Longo, and Survival International, eds., *Decolonizing Conservation.* Philadelphia, PA: Common Notions, pp. 175–177.

Gomez, T. M., M. Guardiola, and P. Ybarra, eds. (2018). Rewilding: Recovery, Remembrances, and Reconnection with the Ancestral Wild. Special Issue. *About Place Journal* 5(1), https://aboutplacejournal.org/issues/rewilding/.

Grant, M. (1916). *The Passing of the Great Race, or, the Racial Basis of European History.* New York: Charles Scribner's Sons.

Gwich'in Steering Committee. (2020). Arctic Indigenous Climate Summit Report: June 10–14, 2019, https://ourarcticrefuge.org/wp-content/uploads/2020/11/aics2019-report-final.pdf.

Gwichya Gwich'in Place Names Project (1993). https://atlas.gwichin.ca/index.html

Harrison, R. P. (2003). *Dominion of the Dead.* Chicago: University of Chicago Press.

Hausdoerffer, J., B. P. Hecht, M. K. Nelson, and K. K. Cummings, eds. (2021). *What Kind of Ancestor Do You Want to Be.* Chicago: University of Chicago Press.

Hernandez, J. (2022). *Fresh Banana Leaves: Healing Indigenous Landscapes through Indigenous Science.* Huichin, unceded Ohlone land aka Berkeley: North Atlantic Books.

Hornaday, W. T. (1913). *Our Vanishing Wildlife: Its Extermination and Preservation*. New York: New York Zoological Society.

Huntingon, E. (In Conjunction with the Directors of the American Eugenics Society). (1935). *Tomorrow's Children; the Goal of Eugenics*. New York: John Wiley & Sons.https://babel.hathitrust.org/cgi/pt?id=mdp.39015034788995&seq=7.

Jackson, W. (2011). *Consulting the Genius of the Place*. Berkeley: Counterpoint.

Kanngieser, A. and Z. Todd. (2020). From Environmental Case Study to Environmental Kin Study. *History and Theory* 59(3): 385–393.

Kaye, R. (2006). *Last Great Wilderness: The Campaign to Establish the Arctic National Wildlife Refuge*. Anchorage: University of Alaska Press.

Kaye, R, P.N. Andrews, B. Demientieff, and L. Carron. (2021). Wilderness and Traditional Indigenous Beliefs: Conflicting or Intersecting Perspectives on the Human-Nature Relationship? *RewildingEarth,* https://rewilding.org/wilderness-and-traditional-indigenous-beliefs-conflicting-or-intersecting-perspectives-on-the-human-nature-relationship/.

Kimmerer, R. (2013). *Braiding Sweetgrass*. Minneapolis: Milkweed Books.

Kolopenuk, J. (2020). Provoking *Bad* Biocitizenship. Pages Special Report: For "All of Us"? On the Weight of Genomic Knowledge. Garrison: Hastings Center, S23–S29.

Komarek, R. (1941). Confidential Report on South Florida Deer-Fever Tick Investigation, *LP 9/25/10-2*, 4(2): 46–53

Langston, N. (2017). The Wisconsin Experiment, *about Places Journal*, https://doi.org/10.22269/170425.

Lanham, J. D. (2016). *The Home Place: Memoirs of a Colored Man's Love Affair with Nature*. Minneapolis: Milkweed Editions.

Lefler, B. J. (2014). Nuwuvi (Southern Paiute) Ecological Knowledge of Piñon-Juniper Woodlands: Implications for Conservation and Sustainable Resource Use in Two Southern Nevada Protected Areas, Portland State University DXScholar, Dissertations and Theses.

Leopold Papers (LP), Madison, University of Wisconsin, UW-Digitized Collections, https://search.library.wisc.edu/digital/AAldoLeopold.

Leopold, A. (1949, 1987). *A Sand County Almanac and Sketches Here and There*. New York: Oxford University Press.

Leopold, A. (1933). *Game Management*. New York: Charles Scribner's Sons.

Leopold, A. (1935). Why the Wilderness Society? *Living Wilderness* 1(1): 6.

Leopold, A. (1946a). Racial Wisdom and Conservation. *Journal of Heredity* 37(9): 275–279.

Leopold, A. (1946b). Erosion as a Menace to the Social and Economic Future of the Southwest. *Journal of Forestry* 44(9): 627–633.

Leopold, A., chairman, L. J. Cole, N. C. Fassett, C. A. Herrick, Chancey Juday, and G. Wagner. (1937). The University and Conservation of Wisconsin Wildlife: Science Inquiry: Publication III. *Bulletin of the University of Wisconsin*, Serial No. 2211, 1–39.

Leopold, L., ed. (1993). *Round River from the Journals of Aldo Leopold*. New York: Oxford University Press.

Lin, Q. F. (2020). Aldo Leopold's Life–Work and the Scholarship It Inspired. *Socio-ecological Practice Research* 2(1): 3–30.

Lin, Q. F. (2014). Aldo Leopold's Unrealized Proposals to Rethink Economics. *Ecological Economics* 108: 104-114.

Long, L. (2017). Tritt-Frank Helps Teach a Village the Value of Education, https://www.uaf.edu/news/archives/news-archives-2010-2021/tritt-frank-helps-teach-a-village-the-value-of-education.php.

Lorbiecki, M. (2016). *A Fierce Green Fire: Aldo Leopold's Life and Legacy*. New York: Oxford University Press.

Malthus, T. R. (1798, 1803). *Parallel Chapters from the First and Second Editions of "An Essay on the Principle of Population."* New York: Macmillan, 1909.

McKibben, B. (2022). *The Flag, the Cross, and the Station Wagon*. New York: Henry Holt.

McLean, S.-A. (2020). Social Constructions, Historical Grounds. *Practicing Anthropology* 42(3): 40–44.

Meine, C. (2010). *Aldo Leopold: His Life and Work*. Madison: University of Wisconsin Press.

Meine, C. (2022). Land, Ethics, Justice, and Aldo Leopold. *Socio-Ecological Practice Research*, 4: 167–187, https://doi.org/10.1007/s42532-022-00117-7.

Memmi, A. (1965). *The Colonizer and the Colonized*. Boston: Beacon Press.

Merchant, C. (1989). *Ecological Revolutions: Nature, Gender, and Science in New England*. Chapel Hill: University of North Carolina Press.

Millstein, R. (2018). Debunking Myths about Leopold's Land Ethic. *Biological Conservation* 217: 391–396

Millstein, R. (2015). Reexamining the Darwinian Basis for Aldo Leopold's Land Ethic. *Ethics, Policy & Environment* 18(3): 301–317.

Mishler, C. and K. Frank. (2019). *Dinjii Vadzaih Dhidlit: The Man Who Became Caribou*. Hanover: IPI.

Morrison, T. (1993). *Playing in the Dark: Whiteness and the Literary Imagination*. New York: Vintage Books.

Mt. Pleasant, J. (2011). The Paradox of the Plows and Productivity: An Agronomic Comparison of Cereal Grain Production under Iroquois Hoe

Culture and European Plow Culture in the Seventeenth and Eighteenth Centuries. *Agricultural History* 85 (4): 460–492.

Nelson, M. (1996). Holists and Fascists and Paper Tigers . . . Oh My! *Ethics and the Environment* 1(2): 103–117.

Nelson, M. and J. B. Callicott. eds. (2008). *The Wilderness Debate Rages On: Continuing the Great New Wilderness Debate*. Athens: University of Georgia Press.

Osborn, F. (1948). *Our Plundered Planet*. Boston: Little Brown.

Pedrotti, F. (2001). Biological Ethics in the Thought of Oscar De Beaux. *Global Bioethics* 14(1): 39–44.

Philip, K. R. (1977). Turmoil at Big Cypress: Seminole Deer and the Florida Cattle Tick Controversy. *The Florida Quarterly* 56(1), Article 5: 1–17.

Powell, M. A. (2016). *Vanishing America: Species Extinction, Racial Peril, and the Origins of Conservation*. Cambridge: Harvard University Press.

Powell, M. A. (2015). "Pestered with Inhabitants": Aldo Leopold, William Vogt, and More Trouble with Wilderness. *Pacific Historical Review* 84(2): 195–226.

Prum, R. (2017). *The Evolution of Beauty: How Darwin's Forgotten Theory of Mate Choice Shapes the Animal World – and Us*. New York: Doubleday.

Raboff, A. P. (2001). Iñuksuk: Northern Koyukon, Gwich'in and Lower Tanana: 1800–1901. Fairbanks: Alaska Native Knowledge Network.

Ribbens, D. (1987). The Making of *a Sand County Almanac*. In J. B. Callicott, ed., *Companion to* a Sand County Almanac. Madison: University of Wisconsin Press, pp. 91–109.

Robinson, D. (2020). *Hungry Listening: Resonant Theory for Indigenous Sound Studies*. Minneapolis: University of Minnesota Press.

Rodríguez, D. (2019). Abolition as Praxis of Human Being: A Forward. *Harvard Law Review* 132(6): 1575–1612.

Rolston, H. (2015). Rediscovering and Rethinking Leopold's Green Fire. *Environmental Ethics* Spring(37): 45–55.

Ruíz, E. and K. Dotson (2017). On the Politics of Coalition: *Feminist Philosophy Quarterly*, 3(2), 1–15, https://doi.org/10.5206/fpq/2017.2.4.

Salwén, H. (2014). The Land Ethic and the Significance of the Fascist Objection. *Ethics, Policy & Environment* 17(2): 192–207.

Savoy, W. (1949). *Alien Land*. Berkeley: E.P. Dutton & Company, Inc.

Savoy, L. (2015). *Trace: History, Race, and the American Landscape*. New York: Counterpoint.

Seidl, I. And C. A. Tisdell. (1999). Carrying Capacity Reconsidered: From Malthus' Population Theory to Cultural Carrying Capacity. *Ecological Economics* 31: 395–408.

Sharkey, E. (ed.) (2023). *A Darker Wilderness: Black Nature Writing from Soil to Stars*. Minneapolis: Milkweed Editions.

Simpson, A. (2018). Why White People Love Franz Boas; or, the Grammar of Indigenous Dispossession. In N. Blackhawk and K. W. Shanley, eds., *Indigenous Visions: Rediscovering the World of Franz Boas*. New Haven: Yale University Press, pp. 166–181.

Simpson, L. B. (2014). Land as Pedagogy: Nishnaabeg Intelligence and Rebellious Transformation. *Decolonization: Indigeneity, Education & Society* 3(3): 1–25.

Smith, J. R. (2021). "Exceeding Beringia": Upending Universal Human Events and Wayward Transits in Arctic Spaces. *Environment and Planning D: Society and Space* 39(1): 158–175.

Sobrevila, C. (2008). *The Role of Indigenous Peoples in Biodiversity Conservation: The Natural but Often Forgoten Parners*. Washington, DC: The World Bank.

Spence, M. D. (1999). *Dispossessing the Wilderness: Indian Removal and the Making of the National Parks*. New York: Oxford University Press.

Starkey, C. (2007). The Land Ethic, Moral Development, and Ecological Rationality. *The Southern Journal of Philosophy* XLV(4): 149–175.

Sultana, F. (2022). The Unbearable Heavinesss of Climate Coloniality. *Political Geography*, www.sciencedirect.com/science/article/abs/pii/S096262982200052X.

Sutter, P. S. (2002). Driven Wild: The Problem of the Wilderness. *Forest History Today* Spring: 2–9.

Taffa, D. (2024). Whiskey Tender: A Memoir. New York: Harper Collins.

Tallbear, K. (2019). Caretaking Relations, Not American Dreaming. *Kalfou* 6(1): 24–41.

Tallbear, K. (2013). *Native American DNA: Tribal Belonging and the False Promise of Genetic Science*. Minneapolis: University of Minnesota Press.

Trethewey, N. (2005). On Whitman, Civil War Memory, and My South. *The Virginia Quarterly Review* 81(2): 50–65.

Tuck, E. and K. W. Yang. (2012). Decolonization Is Not a Metaphor. *Decolonization: Indigeneity, Education and Society* 1(1): 1–40.

Turda, M. (2012). Race, Science, and Eugenics in the Twentieth Century. In A. Bashford and P. Levine, eds., *The Oxford Handbook of the History of Eugenics*. New York: Oxford University Press, pp. 62–79.

Van Horn, G., R. W. Kimmerer, and J. Hausdoerffer, eds. (2021). Kinship Belonging in a World of Relations. Chicago: Center for Humans and Nature.

Vásquez-Fernández, A. and Cash Ahenakew pii tai poo taa. (2020). Resurgence of Relationality: Reflections on Decolonizing and Indigenizing Sustainable Development. *Environmental Sustainability* 43: 65–70.

Vogt, W. (1948). *Road to Survival*. New York: William Sloan Associates.

Warren, J. (2006, 2016). *Aldo Leopold's Odyssey*. Washington, DC: Island Press.

Warren, J. (2008). Science, Recreation, and Leopold's Quest for a Durable Scale. In M. Nelson and J. B. Callicott, eds., *The Wilderness Debate Rages on*. Athens: University of Georgia Press, pp. 97–118.

Warren, J. (2011). Weeds, Seeds, and Shovels: Three Lessons of Two Sisters Living Land Health. *Leopold Outlook Magazine*, 11–16.

Warren, J. (2024). Unsettling Leopoldian Wilderness Values in the Arctic. In A. Anson, K. Keeler, I. Lockhart, and T. Lynch, eds., *Unsettling Environments: Indigenous Sovereignties, Settler Colonialism, Environmental Humanities*. Lincol: University of Nebraska Press (pending)

Warren, L. S. (1993). *The Hunter's Game*. New Haven: Yale University Press.

Whyte, K. P. (2014). A Concern about Shifting Interactions between Indigenous and Nonindigenous Parties in U.S. Climate Adaptation Contexts. *Interdisciplinary Environmental Review* 15(2/3): 114–133, https://papers.ssrn.com/sol3/papers.cfm?abstract_id=2439236.

Whyte, K. P. (2015/2017/2024). How Similar Are Indigenous North American and Leopoldian Environmental Ethics? (Draft available, https://papers.ssrn.com/sol3/papers.cfm?abstract_id=2022038.) In A. Anson, K. Keeler, I. Lockhart, and T. Lynch, eds., *Unsettling Environments: Indigenous Sovereignties, Settler Colonialism, Environmental Humanities*, Lincoln: University of Nebraska Press (pending).

Whyte, K. P. (2015). Indigenous Food Systems, Environmental Justice, and Settler-Industrial States. In M. Rawlinson and C. Ward, eds., *Global Food, Global Justice: Essays on Eating under Globalization*. Newcastle upon Tyne: Cambridge Scholars, pp. 143–156.

Whyte, K. P. (2017a). Our Ancestors Dystopia Now: Indigenous Conservation and the Anthropocene. In U. Heise, J. Christensen, and M. Niemann, eds., *The Routledge Companion to the Environmental Humanities*. New York: Routledge, pp. 206–215.

Whyte, K. P. (2017b). Indigenous Climate Change Studies: Indigenizing Futures, Decolonizing the Anthropocene. *English Language Notes* 55(1 (2): 153–162.

Whyte, K. P. (2018b). Indigenous Science (Fiction) for the Anthropocene: Ancestral Dystopias and Fantasies of Climate Change Crisis. *Environment & Planning E: Nature and Space* 1(1–2): 224–242.

Whyte, K. P. (2018a). Settler Colonialism, Ecology, and Environmental Injustice. *Environment and Society: Advances in Research* 9: 125–144.

Whyte, K. P. (2020). Indigenous Environmental Justice: Anti-Colonial Action through Kinship. In B. Coolsaet, ed., *Environmental Justice: Key Issues*. London: Routledge Imprint, pp. 266–278.

Whyte, K. P., Caldwell, C., and Schaefer, M. (2018). Indigenous Lessons About Sustainability Are Not Just for "All Humanity." in J. Sze, ed. Sustainability: Approaches to Environmental Justice and Social Power. New York:: NYU Press.

Wolfe, P. (2006). Settler Colonialism and the Elimination of the Native. *Journal of Genocide Research* 8(4): 387–409.

Ybarra, P. (2022). The Idea of Wilderness to Mexican Americans. In E. H. Allen, ed., *First and Wildest: The Gila Wilderness at 100*. Salt Lake City: Torrey House Press, 29–35.

Ybarra, P. (2016). *Writing the Good Life: Mexican American Literature and the Environment*. Tucson: University of Arizona Press.

Acknowledgments

This work emerges thanks to labors of many Indigenous grassroots organizers and academics. Following from my earlier fossil fuel divestment activism, I participated in advocacy trainings, camps, and grassroots-justice organizing led by Alaska Native women. This honor of participating has changed me. I am grateful to many educators, colleagues, and friends of Native Movement, the Gwich'in Steering Committee, Sovereign Iñupiat for a Living Arctic along with settler colleagues of Northern Alaska Environmental Center and Fairbanks Climate Action Coalition, the latter with whom I served as a council member from 2017–2019. Through what I have begun un/learning from/with you and others – particularly lower Tanana Dene, Dena'ina, and Gwich'in geographies – I acknowledge how my past scholarship and mindset are troubling. I recognize many offenses of my historic work, particularly, in leaving the woven-in white supremacy unchallenged with the force of violent, unjust consequences. Thank you for helping me to do better. I hope that my present and future work can increasingly help support each others' as we continue ahead together in strengthening coalitions and communities grounded in justice, which belongs to love.

In particular, Enei Begaye (Diné and Tohono O'odham), Elisabeth Balster Dabney (settler), Bernadette Demientieff (Gwich'yaa Zhee Gwich'in), Jessica Girard (settler), Tristan Glowa (settler), Princess Daazhraii Johnson (Neets'aii Gwich'in), Shawna Larson (Ahtna and Sugpiaq), Siqiñiq Maupin (Iñupiaq), Odin Miller (settler), Christina Kk'odohdaatlno Edwin (Denaa and Chicana), Nutaaq Simmonds (Iñupiaq), Cathy Walling (settler), Erica Watson (settler) – from my deepest parts, thank you for trainings, conversations, turns of phrases, challenges, and questions, for just being who you are, for being my teachers, for growing and healing in relation, protecting Land, and decolonizing "Alaska" with rippling consequences. Thank you to this Land.

My above un/learning converges with the simmering effects of having read, for me, the re-orienting essay by philosopher, environmental justice organizer, and Potawatomi relative Dr. Kyle Powys Whyte – "How Similar Are Indigenous North American and Leopoldian Environmental Ethics?" Deep thanks, Kyle, for this essay of yours that emerged, years ago, after an NEH Summer Institute where we met. And, immense thanks for your many other brilliant and transformational writings (see https://kylewhyte.seas.umich.edu/articles/), for your time, honesty, and valuing respectfulness. Your expertise along with steadfastness in respect and caring unexpectedly effected an oasis of healing within the too-often hurtful reaches of academic norms. A huge and warm thank you for your framework, for reviewing drafts, for our conversations, and for facilitating a working group of mutually supportive scholars with overlapping and intersecting interests. I sometimes still pinch myself, with gratitude.

My ongoing thanks to this group of amazing colleagues, including Dina Gilio-Whitaker, Jane Mt. Pleasant, Noah Schlager, and Priscilla Ybarra. Each of your frontlines scholarship, sharing of knowledges and sources, and conversations have been re/generative personally and professionally, helping guide my revising of this writing and much more. Speaking as a white, abled, middle-class, settler-colonizer, cis-gender woman, that is, speaking within several currently dominating norms that grant me many privileges, to get to know one's self as neither innocent nor alone in decolonizing, anti-race/ist un/learning work is a most profound gift.

Noah Schlager, Yale's announcement of your talk, "Hard to Catch: Unpacking F&ES's Colonial History," revealed how I still felt on guard in some ways about this process. Afterward, your arguments, evidence, and thesis helped move me more wholly into my responsibilities to join in such unpacking. Thank you for that, and, with respect for your many complementary, ongoing works as a Mvskoke-Creek, Florida Catawba/Cheraw, Jewish and Euro-American descendant and writer, deconstructing colonial legacies within Western conservation, and, in practice, also creating space for Indigenous food sovereignty.

I am grateful for meeting and witnessing your standing-up, Dr. Jane Mt. Pleasant. Hearing you bring decolonization into a conference setting where this was, indeed, unsettling prompted vigorous, durable, and educational conversations. These include reflecting on the power of grammatical article – "the." I admire your research career as a woman of Tuscarora ancestry focusing on Indigenous agriculture with contemporary relevance at Cornell, where you are now emeritus. Over these years, thank you for sharing important sources with me, including ones relevant to Stockbridge-Munsee Community Band of Mohican Indians' lands colonized by my European-settler family who, then, also impoverished them and ourselves via unsustainable farming practices. Since my family legacy includes the post-Civil War naturalist-writer John Burroughs, your work also has been helpful in revisiting the power of his platform. That is, helpful in revisiting Burroughs, who, with large-heartedness, encouraged settlers to become intimate home-lovers. Yet, this new rooting was in stolen Lands while ruthlessly erasing recently removed, sovereign Indigenous Nations and genocide. Land Back.

I wish to honor the many works of the Chicanx feminist writer and literature professor Dr. Priscilla Ybarra, including your *Writing the Good Life: Mexican American Literature and the Environment*, which continues to permeate and remake the environmental humanities and environmental movements. Over the years, hearing you speak and getting to cross paths at various conferences, too, has opened doors for me respecting Chicanx Land-based histories, ethics, and knowledges as crucial for coalition-building and habitable futures. And, I have a lot more to learn. I am most eager for your ongoing work, including a book-in-progress, which, as I understand, develops not only the environmental but also the Mexican American legacy of the Aldo and Estella Leopold family in relation to colonialism, capitalism, and white supremacy.

With warm respect, Dina Gilio-Whitaker – scholar, author, educator, independent consultant, and Colville Confederated Tribes descendant – thank you for your several volumes, including your book *As Long as Grass Grows: The Indigenous Fight for Environmental Justice from Colonization to Standing Rock*. Your luminary work is essential for understanding how white supremacy and patriarchy weave with U.S. settler conservation. During these Covid years, I have learned also from your bold insights in many webinars and talks across many venues. Please accept my heartfelt gratitude for your thoughtfulness and consideration in our ongoing conversations. I deeply appreciate your rigor, clear-sightedness in action and kindness all along the way, forging onward with this manuscript and beyond and besides it. Thank you.

I want to add a warm note to Dr. Lauret Savoy, geologist, author, and woman of African American, Euro-American, and Native American heritage. I have been blessed to share some (too little) time and spaces with you over the years. Thank you for your deep, complex, vanguard work, including *Trace: Memory, History, Race, and the American Landscape*). Yet, it wasn't until a couple of years ago that I carefully read your father's book, *Alien Land*, published in 1949 as was *A Sand County Almanac*. For remembrance and ongoing consideration of what it says to do so, I indeed now shelve them cover-to-cover and in plain view.

A special thank you to my partner, Dr. Jim Warren, English and environmental literature and culture scholar, educator, multi-book author, vocational-community coordinator, and outdoor guide, for his close readings, very very patient listening, suggestions, copy-editing in earlier drafts, and encompassing care. Thank you also for the particulars of walking with the dog and bringing me firewood and ice cream.

Much gratitude also to Elisabeth Dabney, already mentioned above, Executive Director of the Northern Alaska Environmental Center and literary agent and editor, for her close-reading and copy-editing in earlier drafts.

Thank you to Jonathan Cobb, my editor for *Aldo Leopold's Odyssey,* whom I still call my friend. Without his attentive expertise and kind patience my words would have meant far less, for better or worse! Thank you, Island Press!

Acknowledgments

In 2019–2020 I was an Ecosphere Studies collaborator and visiting scholar at The Land Institute in Salina, Kansas, occupying Lands of sovereign Kaw/Kansa and neighboring Nations and Tribes. I thank The Land Institute for support during that year, which helped me complete a first draft of this work in January 2020. I thank them, too, for the opportunity soon thereafter to discuss parts of that draft with TLI's community while in residence. In particular, I am grateful to Dr. Aubrey Streit-Krug, environmental humanities writer and teacher, collaborator on an Omaha language and culture textbook, literary ethnobotanist, and TLI's Ecosphere Studies Director, and now TLI's Director of Perennial Cultures Lab. Thank you, Aubrey, for our many and continuing vigorous and thought-provoking conversations and warm times hosted in your company. Thank you for your friendship.

I also continue to thank the Center for Humans and Nature and their president, Dr. Brooke Parry Hecht, with whom I have served as a Senior Scholar and ongoing, appointed Fellow. Thank you for your support. Dear thanks to CHN Managing Editor Katherine Kassouf Cummings, Lebanese-American writer and musician, and enduring, encouraging friend.

A special, warm thanks to scholars Dr. Mary Evelyn Tucker and Dr. John Grim of the Yale Forum on Religion and Ecology for your unrelenting support with opportunities to try out and share ideas, including some of this work, in classrooms and community. May fields keep opening, with much love.

This May (2024), I graduated with an MFA in Creative Writing from the Institute of American Indian Arts. I could not be more grateful or more myself. Huge thanks to you Debra Taffa for believing in, welcoming, and mentoring me with your incisive, gentle, and intuitive ways. Deepest thanks to each of my mentors – to Layli Long Soldier for guiding me, for just the right touch, for "elegance," and so many generosities.; and to Chip Livingston with whom I was working when revisions for this Element and work on my MFA manuscript and craft essay collided. Your insights on my creative work overflowed into helping me do better in this more academic one. Thank you! And thank you to Kimberly Blaeser, two time workshop facilitator, for all manner of conversations and warm care. Thank you for helping me become a more sensitive and more clear writer while honoring ambiguity. I respect your labor as a former member of The Aldo Leopold Foundation board of directors, with my awareness past due. And to my many dear student colleagues. I miss you! And, look, here it is! Now back to my beloved ʻɛkoʊ and birdsong, and who knows what. All writing is a creative path.

I am grateful indeed to more than I can name whose influences have helped to precipitate and inform this season of living and to generate this particular work.

In addition to those mentioned above, I respectfully acknowledge Susan Abasa, Cindy Adams, John Adams, Samuel Alexander, Tom Alworth, Marco Armiero, Jeannette Armstrong, Heather Aruffo, Nadine Barnicle, Charley Basham, Noelle Blanc, Carl Bowden, Kjersti Bowen, Lisa Brooks, Heather Bruegl, Susan Campbell, Terry Chapin, Bathsheba Demuth, Finis Dunaway, Gretel Ehrlich, Robert S. Emmett, Erin Marie Espelie, Bonnie Etherington, Kate Evans, Jamie Figueroa, Susan Flader, Betty Flitt, Margaret Forster, Jimmy Fox, Daniel Geller, Adrienne Ghaly, Raquel Gutiérrez, Debra Gwartney, Kerri Hamos, John Hausdoerffer, Chase Hensel, Ursula Heise, Betty Holley, Mickey Houlihan, Pam Houston, Aerin Hyun, Wes Jackson, Dale Jamieson, Willis Jenkins, Len Kamerling, Julie Kaufman, Toni Kaufman, Robin Kimmerer, Dave Klein, Piyush Labhsetwar, Nancy Langston, Jan Lokken, Sophie Lasoff, Mary Beth Leigh, John Linstrom, Barry Lopez, Pamela Lovis, Cedar Lutz, Rebecca Lutz, Fred Lutzi, John Manthei, Ryan Marsh, Ian Marshall, Phil Marshall, Joan McGregor, Bill McKibben, Curt Meine, Carolyn Merchant, Gregg Mitman, Kathleen Dean Moore, Phyllis Morrow, Patrick Nunnally, Sharon Olds, Hishinlai' Peter, Diane Preston, Lucy Quimby, Carol Raffensperger, Justin Raymond, Belinda Rodriguez, Caroline Roche, Mike Roche, Phoebe Rohrbacher, Dante Ruiz, Dave Salmon, Jane Salmon, Karen Salmon, Toby Salmon, Laura Sanford, Siobhan Senier, Dan Shilling, Nutaaq Simmonds, Kim Tallbear, Monty Thompson, Luke Titus, John Toya, Martha Toya, Marina Tsaplina, Brie Van Dam, Carol Van Deelen, Tim Van Deelen, Gavin Van Horn, Vivian Wadlin, Laura Walls, Carl Wallman, Kennedy Warne, Annie Wenstrup, Phil Wight, Terry Tempest Williams, and Christiana Zenner.

Special and deep thanks to the series editors of *Cambridge Elements: Elements in Indigenous Environmental Research*: Dina Gilio-Whitaker, Clint Carroll, Joy Porter, and, particularly, Associate Editor, Matthias Wong. Thank you for your careful and skillful attention, fortitude, and kindness in our exchanges, and for seeing me and this Element through. Thank you. Thank you Shalini Priyatharshini for your gracious support, and that of copyeditors, typesetters and staff. Thank you for the honor to publish in this amazing venue. I cannot imagine a better home for this work. I am profoundly grateful.

Thank you to two anonymous reviewers. Responding to your comments pushed me to refocus and/or strengthen this work in substantive ways.

I feel, acutely, that this Element must be imperfect, in seen and as-yet unseen ways. Any remaining mistakes and offenses remain my responsibility. I will continue my un/learning journey, deeply revising my work and life, responsively and openly.

Research Ethics Statement

All stories and quotations of Alaska Native storytellers are either from published and/or public sources, which are cited, or heard by the author, in-person, and included only with the storytellers' explicit consent, also cited.

Cambridge Elements

Indigenous Environmental Research

Series Editors
Dina Gilio-Whitaker
California State University San Marcos

Dina Gilio-Whitaker (Colville Confederated Tribes) is a lecturer of American Indian Studies at California State University San Marcos, and an independent educator in American Indian environmental policy and other issues. She teaches courses on environmentalism and American Indians, traditional ecological knowledge, religion and philosophy, Native women's activism, American Indians and sports, and decolonization. Dina is the award-winning *As Long as Grass Grows: The Indigenous Fight for Environmental Justice* (Beacon Press, 2019). She is also an award-winning journalist, with her work appearing in *Indian Country Today*, the *Los Angeles Times*, *Time.com*, *The Boston Globe*, and many more.

Clint R. Carroll
University of Colorado Boulder

Clint Carroll is an Associate Professor in the Department of Ethnic Studies at the University of Colorado Boulder. A citizen of the Cherokee Nation, he works at the intersections of Indigenous studies, anthropology, and political ecology. His first book, *Roots of Our Renewal: Ethnobotany and Cherokee Environmental Governance* (University of Minnesota Press, 2015), explores how tribal natural resource managers navigate the material and structural conditions of settler colonialism, and how recent efforts in cultural revitalization inform such practices through traditional Cherokee governance and local environmental knowledge. He is an active member of the Native American and Indigenous Studies Association and the Society for Applied Anthropology. He also serves on the editorial boards for *Cultural Anthropology* and *Environment and Society*.

Joy Porter
University of Birmingham

Joy Porter is University of Birmingham 125th Anniversary Chair, Professor of Indigenous and Environmental History and Principal Investigator of the Treatied Spaces Research Group. She is the Principal Investigator for "Brightening the Covenant Chain: Revealing Cultures of Diplomacy Between the Iroquois and the British Crown" (2021–2025) and "Historic Houses Global Connections: Revisioning Two Northern Ireland Historic Houses and Estates" (2024–2027). Joy has over 65 publications, including four research monographs and three other books. She received the Wordcraft Circle of Native Writers Writer of the Year Award for *The Cambridge Companion to Native American Literature* (Cambridge University Press, 2005) and a Choice Outstanding Academic Title Award for *To be Indian: The Life of Iroquois-Seneca Arthur Caswell Parker* (Oklahoma, 2023, 2001). Her latest book is *Trauma, Primitivism and the First World War: The Making of Frank Prewett* (Bloomsbury, 2021). She was born in Derry, in the North of Ireland.

Associate Editor
Matthias Wong
National University of Singapore

Matthias Wong is Senior Tutor at the National University of Singapore and an Associate of the Treatied Spaces Research Group at the University of Birmingham. His research is in the environmental humanities, specifically in the use of digital methods to recover Indigenous presence in historical sources such as maps and treaties, and in reconnecting Indigenous collections in museums with their source communities. He co-leads the "Green Toolkit for a New Space Economy" project, which aims to widen the space sector's understanding of sustainability to include the cultural and social dimensions. His collaborators include King's Digital Lab at King's College London, The Alan Turing Institute, and Nordamerika Native Museum Zurich. His research interests are on the process of meaning-making, particularly in understanding senses of time and place, and on the repercussions of trauma and disruption. His research on early modern futurity has been published in *Historical Research*, and he teaches courses on cultural astronomy, public history, and digital history.

Advisory Board

Ann McGrath, *Australian National University*
Camilla Brattland, *Arctic University of Norway (UIT)*
Dalo Njera, *Mzuzu University*
Kalpana Giri, *The Regional Community Forestry Training Center for Asia and the Pacific (RECOFTC)*
Simone Athayde, *Florida International University*
Joe Bryan, *University of Colorado Boulder*
Kanyinke Sena, *Egerton University*
Kyle Powys Whyte, *University of Michigan*
Dale Turner, *University of Toronto*
Michael Hathaway, *Simon Fraser University*
Paige West, *Columbia University*
Pratik Chakrabarti, *University of Houston*
Rauna Kuokkanen, *University of Lapland*
Shannon Speed, *University of California Los Angeles*
Mike Dockry, *University of Minnesota*

About the Series

Elements in Indigenous Environmental Research offers state-of-the-art interdisciplinary analyses within the rapidly growing area of Indigenous environmental research. The series investigates how environmental issues and processes relate to Indigenous socio-economic, cultural and political dynamics.

Cambridge Elements ≡

Indigenous Environmental Research

Elements in the Series

Defending Community, Territory, and Indigenous Environmental Relations
Levi Gahman, Filiberto Penados, Cristina Coc and Shelda-Jane Smith

"Alaska" Is Not a Blank Space: Unsettling Aldo Leopold's Odyssey
Julianne Warren

A full series listing is available at: www.cambridge.org/EIER

For EU product safety concerns, contact us at Calle de José Abascal, 56–1°,
28003 Madrid, Spain or eugpsr@cambridge.org.